GRAN'S SOUP

A Ham Hock
  & boiled for 3 hours

- lift Hock out
- Cup of split peas.
- Cup of lentils.
- Big bit of turnip.
- Big potato
- 2 carrots
- 2 onions.
- 5 celery sticks.
- small leek

- Simmer slowly for about 2 hours
 - liquidize.

Quick & Easy
Students' Cookbook

Quick & Easy Students' Cookbook

Molly Perham

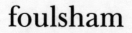

foulsham

LONDON • NEW YORK • TORONTO • SYDNEY

foulsham

Bennetts Close, Cippenham, Berkshire SL1 5AP

for Daniel and Justin

ISBN 0-572-01805-3
Copyright © 1993 Molly Perham

Typeset by Jeffery White Creative Associates, Oxford, UK.

Printed and bound in Great Britain by
Cox & Wyman Ltd, Reading, Berkshire.

contents

the BASICS

cooking methods

One of the problems of fending for yourself is that you almost certainly won't have access to a well-equipped, modern kitchen. It will far more likely be an ancient cooker shared with other people – or a single gas ring on the floor by the fire. For the recipes in this book I have indicated whether they are cooked on top of the stove (or on the gas ring) or in the oven, so that you know before you start whether you have the necessary facilities at your disposal. Food is cooked either with water (boiling, steaming, stewing) or dry (frying, grilling (broiling), roasting, baking).

boiling

The food to be cooked is put in a saucepan and covered with water. Depending on the type of food, the water may be boiling or cold. The correct way to cook most vegetables, for example, is to put them into a saucepan and add enough boiling water to cover them, with a little salt. Put the pan on a hot plate or gas ring and heat until the water is bubbling and giving off steam. Then reduce the heat to low and let the vegetables simmer until they are soft and ready to eat. The saucepan should have a well-fitting lid to prevent the water evaporating. Old potatoes are best covered in cold water and then brought to the boil.

Rice and pasta are cooked by putting them into a pan of boiling water with a little salt added. Make sure there is plenty of water because much of it will be absorbed.

steaming

Food is cooked in the steam that rises from a pan of boiling water, in a container with a perforated base. A well-fitting lid is essential. A steamer is useful for cooking a whole meal if you have only a single gas ring. Two or more perforated containers can be stood on top of one another to cook different foods at the same time. This is a good way to cook vegetables because less of the soluble nutrients in the food are lost. A fillet of fish can be steamed by putting it between two plates over a saucepan of boiling water.

stewing

This is a long, slow method of cooking that makes even the toughest meat digestible. The food is cooked slowly in a small quantity of water or other liquid (stock, beer, etc). The advantages of stewing are that you can use cheap cuts of meat; that the soluble nutrients go into the liquid so that no food value is lost; that wonderful flavours develop in the liquid; and, once prepared, a stew will cook happily with no more attention.

frying

This is a quick method of cooking, and can be done in three ways – shallow frying, deep frying and dry frying. The fat or oil that you use must be capable of being heated to a high temperature. Vegetable and sunflower oils are suitable, or lard, but margarine and butter are not. Before starting to fry the fat must be heated to the right temperature. If it is too cool, the food will absorb fat and be horribly greasy. Fat that is too hot will burn and give the food a bitter flavour – or even catch alight so that you have a blazing frying pan (skillet) to cope with. At the right temperature the fat will have a faint haze rising from the surface. When you have finished frying, leave the pan to cool down slightly and then pour the fat into a clean bowl. It can be kept in the fridge to use again.

Shallow frying is suitable for anything that is thin enough to cook through by turning on both sides – eggs, fish fingers, steak, mushrooms, sliced onions, etc. Stir-fry dishes are cooked in this way.

Deep frying is necessary for chips (French fries), and food cooked in batter such as fish, chicken nuggets, and apple fritters. The pan used for deep frying has a frying basket so that you can lift the cooked food from the hot fat. You should put in only enough chips (or whatever) to cover the bottom of the basket, otherwise the fat will cool and you will get soggy chips. Drain the food on kitchen paper before serving.

In *dry frying* the fat is gently extracted from the food being cooked – such as bacon or sausages – and no extra fat is added.

The advantage of frying is that it is quick. The disadvantages are that too much fried food is not good for you, and that frying can be dangerous. Boiling fat is highly inflammable. If the pan catches fire cover it with something to exclude the air. **NEVER** throw on water.

11

grilling (broiling)

Grilling (broiling), like frying, is a quick way of cooking and is suitable for small, fairly thin food such as chops, cutlets, steaks, bacon, sausages, fish fingers and tomatoes. It is best to start the food under a hot grill (broiler) to seal the surface and then reduce the heat to cook through more gently, turning the food over occasionally. Bread, buns and crumpets can be toasted under the grill if you don't have a toaster.

roasting

For roasting you need an oven, and this method of cooking is suitable for joints of meat or whole chickens. Only good quality, tender meat can be cooked like this – leg or shoulder of lamb, leg or loin of pork, sirloin or topside of beef – otherwise it will be tough to eat.

baking

Baking is also done in an oven, and usually refers to bread, cake, pastries, pizzas, or things like potatoes or apples.

● *Other methods of cooking food described in this book are microwaving (see page 100) and slow-cooking (see page 148).*

● *A sandwich toaster costs less than £20 and is ideal for making quick hot snacks.*

equipment

It's possible to create all kinds of interesting meals with the minimum of equipment. The trick is to buy things that have many different uses. Make sure that they are suitable for what you intend to use them for: for the oven or grill (broiler) you need heatproof dishes (such as Pyrex), otherwise they will break. Some saucepans are particularly recommended for either gas or electricity, and you can now buy cooking equipment that can be used both on top of the stove and in the oven.

If you buy new equipment there will be instructions about how to clean it. Otherwise, abrasive (e.g. Brillo) pads clean all but the most heavily-burnt saucepans – but never use them on non-stick surfaces. If you always fill a saucepan in which you have cooked scrambled eggs, milk, etc. with water and leave it to soak, it will be easier to clean when you fish it out of the sink two weeks later.

The following is what you will need for cooking most of the dishes in this book:

1 large non-stick frying pan (skillet), with a lid
Use for stir-fries, pancakes, rissotto, and all kinds of other dishes, as well as frying.

1 small frying pan (skillet) or omelette pan

1 large and 1 small saucepan, with lids

2 ovenproof (e.g. Pyrex) casserole dishes, 1 large and 1 small, with lids
Use for casseroles, puddings, mixing, serving salads, storing things in the refrigerator – the list is endless.

1 ovenproof roasting dish
Also use for puddings, lasagna, etc.

1 ovenproof measuring jug

Also use for gravy, custard, etc.

Baking tray
Use for pizzas, biscuits, buns, scones, sausage rolls, etc.

Metal sieve
Plastic melts.

Cheese grater
The box kind has different types of grater on each of the four sides.

Tin opener

Bottle opener

Fish slice (pancake turner)

Wooden spoon
Metal ones get hot while cooking.

Sharp chopping knife

Chopping board

Tablespoon, dessertspoon, teaspoon
For measuring flour, rice, sugar, etc if you don't have scales.

Dinner plate, teaplate, breakfast bowl, mug, egg cup, knife, fork, spoon
More of these if you intend to share your meals with anyone.

The following items are very nice to have if you can afford it, or if someone wants to give you a useful present:

Wok
Pepper mill
Scales
Slow cooker
Sandwich toaster
Wide-necked flask (for making yoghurt)

the B *s*

beans

Beans and peas, or pulses, have become much more popular recently, and you don't have to be a vegetarian to enjoy them. They are ideal food for people on a low budget because they are inexpensive, filling, and nutritious. Pulses are high in fibre and protein, and also contain important vitamins and minerals such as vitamin B, iron and phosphorus – and they don't contain any saturated fat. You can add them to soups and stews to make a more filling meal, use them as a salad ingredient – or as a substitute for meat. Even the most determined meat-eater will enjoy the recipes below.

Supermarkets now stock a wide range of both dried and canned beans. The dried ones are cheaper, but they require more effort because most of them need to be soaked for several hours and then cooked before using them. Pulses yield double their dried weight

15

when cooked, so you need to take this into account when calculating quantities.

1 ▪ baked beans

The original baked beans were a type of haricot bean called 'navy', prepared with a tomato sauce. Baked beans on toast is a very healthy meal, as it provides both pulse and cereal proteins, and is low in fat. You can now buy tins of baked beans that are low in sugar and salt, too.

Here are some other ideas for serving baked beans:

Baked beans and bacon
Chop a rasher (slice) of bacon into small pieces, fry until crisp, then add baked beans and heat through.

Baked beans and garlic sausage
Skin and chop a piece of garlic sausage and add to baked beans before warming them.

Baked beans and cheese
Put beans in a heatproof dish, top with a couple of tablespoons grated Cheddar cheese, and put under the grill (broiler) until the cheese melts and starts to bubble.

Curried baked beans
Slice a small onion, fry in a little oil until soft, stir in $1/2$ teaspoon curry powder, then add the baked beans, stir well and heat through.

2 ▪ butter beans (Lima or fava)

These large, cream-coloured beans have a sweetish flavour and a soft, floury texture. The dried ones should be soaked for 3–4 hours and then cooked for at least an hour. Butter beans are good in salads and stews.

tuna and butter bean salad

Servings: 1
Time to prepare: 2 minutes

Ingredients	Metric	Imperial	American
small tin tuna fish	*1*	*1*	*1*
tin butter (Lima or fava) beans (or 50g/2oz dried, cooked)	*200g*	*7oz*	*7oz*
a little French dressing			

Equipment
Sieve, small bowl

Cooking method
No cooking required

1 Drain and flake the tuna fish.
2 Drain the beans into a sieve and rinse well in cold water.
3 Mix tuna fish and beans with a little French dressing.
4 Eat with crusty bread and a green salad.

butter beans in cheese sauce

Servings: 1
Time to prepare: 10 minutes

This is good eaten with brown rice.

Ingredients	Metric	Imperial	American
tin butter (Lima or fava) beans	*200g*	*7oz*	*7oz*
natural yoghurt	*2 tbsp*	*2 tbsp*	*2 tbsp*
grated Cheddar cheese	*50g*	*2oz*	*$^1/_2$ cup*

Equipment
Saucepan

Cooking method
Top of stove

1 Heat the beans in a saucepan, then drain off the liquid.
2 Stir in the yoghurt and continue heating gently.
3 Finally, add the cheese and continue heating until it melts.

3 ▪ chick peas (garbanzo beans)

These are pale golden hard peas that look rather like hazelnuts. When cooked they have a rich nutty flavour. Chick peas (garbanzo beans) are very versatile, so it's a good idea to keep a tin in your cupboard. Dried ones need more soaking than any of the other pulses – it's best to leave them overnight in plenty of cold water. In the morning rinse thoroughly and put into a saucepan with fresh water. Boil rapidly for 10 minutes, removing any foam that rises to the surface, then reduce the heat, cover and simmer for at least an hour, until the peas are soft. Salt should always be added at the end of cooking: if you add it earlier it will make the skins tough.

chick pea stew

Servings: 1
Time to prepare: 15 minutes

Ingredients	Metric	Imperial	American
tin chick peas (garbanzo beans) (or 100g/4oz dried, cooked)	200g	7oz	7oz
oil	1 tbsp	1 tbsp	1 tbsp
small onion	1	1	1
garlic clove	1	1	1
green (bell) pepper	1/2	1/2	1/2
red (bell) pepper	1/2	1/2	1/2
a piece of garlic sausage	50g	2oz	2oz
salt and pepper			
natural yoghurt	2 tbsp	2 tbsp	2 tbsp

Equipment
Saucepan, sieve, chopping board, knife

Cooking method
Top of stove

1 Heat the oil in a saucepan.
2 Peel and slice the onion and garlic and fry gently in the oil for 2–3 minutes.
3 Deseed and slice the peppers and add to the saucepan. Fry for another 2–3 minutes.
4 Add the drained chick peas (garbanzo beans) and sliced garlic sausage.
5 Season with salt and pepper.
6 Simmer gently for 10 minutes.
7 Stir in the yoghurt and continue cooking gently until the stew has thickened.
8 Eat with crusty bread.

spicy chick peas with tomato

Servings: 2
Time to prepare: 25 minutes

Half of this dish can be eaten warm with rice, pasta or crusty bread, and the rest saved to eat cold as part of a salad.

Ingredients

Ingredients	Metric	Imperial	American
tin chick peas (garbanzo beans) (or 100g/4oz dried, cooked)	*200g*	*7oz*	*7oz*
vegetable oil	*2 tbsp*	*2 tbsp*	*2 tbsp*
small onion	*1*	*1*	*1*
clove of garlic	*1*	*1*	*1*
turmeric	*$^1/_2$ tsp*	*$^1/_2$ tsp*	*$^1/_2$ tsp*
paprika	*$^1/_2$ tsp*	*$^1/_2$ tsp*	*$^1/_2$ tsp*
ground cumin	*$^1/_2$ tsp*	*$^1/_2$ tsp*	*$^1/_2$ tsp*
ground coriander	*$^1/_2$ tsp*	*$^1/_2$ tsp*	*$^1/_2$ tsp*
garam masala	*$^1/_2$ tsp*	*$^1/_2$ tsp*	*$^1/_2$ tsp*
tomatoes	*2*	*2*	*2*
salt and black pepper			

Equipment
Saucepan, sieve, chopping board, knife

Cooking method
Top of stove

1 Heat the oil in a saucepan.
2 Peel and slice the onion and garlic. Fry in the oil for about 5 minutes, until soft.
3 Add the spices and continue frying for another 2 minutes, stirring all the time.
4 Chop the tomatoes and add to the saucepan. Continue cooking until the tomatoes are soft.
5 Drain and add the chick peas (garbanzo beans). Stir well.

6 Cook gently for another 5 minutes.
7 Season with salt and pepper.

chick pea curry

Servings: 1
Time to prepare: 15 minutes

Ingredients	Metric	Imperial	American
tin chick peas (garbanzo beans) (or 100g/4oz dried, cooked)	200g	7oz	7oz
onion	1	1	1
vegetable oil	1 tbsp	1 tbsp	1 tbsp
curry powder	1 tsp	1 tsp	1 tsp
tin chopped tomatoes	200g	7oz	7oz
natural yoghurt (optional)	2 tbsp	2 tbsp	2 tbsp

Equipment
Saucepan, sieve, chopping board, knife

Cooking method
Top of stove

1 Heat the oil in a saucepan.
2 Peel and slice the onion and fry gently in the oil for about 5 minutes, until soft.
3 Add the curry powder and cook for another minute, stirring constantly.
4 Add the tinned tomatoes and drained chick peas (garbanzo beans) and continue cooking for another 5 minutes, until everything is heated through.
5 Add the yoghurt just before serving.
6 Eat with rice.

4 ▪ black-eyed beans

These small, kidney-shaped beans are cream-coloured with a distinctive black spot where they were joined to the pod. The dried ones should be soaked for 3–4 hours and then cooked for 1–1$\frac{1}{2}$ hours.

5 ▪ borlotti beans

These are Italian beans with a bitter-sweet flavour, used in recipes such as *pasta e fagioli* (pasta and bean soup) and minestrone. They are attractive to look at – oval-shaped and quite plump, with a pinkish-brown skin and maroon streaks – so they look good in mixed bean salads like the one below. The dried ones should be soaked for 3–4 hours and then cooked for 1–1$\frac{1}{2}$ hours.

6 ▪ cannellini beans

These are also known as Italian haricot beans or white kidney beans. They are creamy-white and fairly slender and have a nice, subtle flavour. The dried ones should be soaked for 3–4 hours and then cooked for 2 hours.

mixed bean salad

Servings: 2–3
Time to prepare: 10 minutes

This salad can be eaten warm, and the rest saved to eat cold at a later meal.

Ingredients	Metric	Imperial	American
olive or sunflower oil	2 tbsp	2 tbsp	2 tbsp
lemon juice	1 tbsp	1 tbsp	1 tbsp
clear honey	1 tsp	1 tsp	1 tsp
chopped fresh herbs, (or 1 teaspoon dried herbs)	1 tbsp	1 tbsp	1 tbsp
tin chick peas (garbanzo beans) (or 100g/4oz dried, cooked)	200g	7oz	7oz
tin black-eyed or borlotti beans (or100g/4oz dried, cooked)	200g	7oz	7oz
tomato	1	1	1
small onion	1	1	1
small green (bell) pepper	1	1	1
olives (optional)	5	5	5

Equipment
Saucepan, sieve, chopping board, knife

Cooking method
Top of stove

1 Put oil, lemon juice, honey and herbs into a saucepan and heat gently for 2 minutes.
2 Drain the chick peas (garbanzo beans) and beans and add to the saucepan.
3 Stir until they are heated through.
4 Slice the tomato, onion and green pepper and add to the saucepan.
5 Heat for another minute.
6 Remove from heat and add the olives if you are using them.

bean and pasta stew

Servings: 1–2
Time to prepare: 10 minutes

Ingredients	Metric	Imperial	American
tin cannellini or borlotti beans	*200g*	*7oz*	*7oz*
tin tomatoes	*200g*	*7oz*	*7oz*
tomato purée (paste) or sauce	*1 tbsp*	*1 tbsp*	*1 tbsp*
oil	*1 tbsp*	*1 tbsp*	*1 tbsp*
small onion	*1*	*1*	*1*
clove garlic	*1*	*1*	*1*
a handful of pasta shapes	*50g*	*2oz*	*¹/₂ cup*
chopped parsley (or 1 teaspoon dried herbs)	*1 tbsp*	*1 tbsp*	*1 tbsp*

Equipment
Saucepan, sieve, chopping board, knife

Cooking method
Top of stove

1 Heat the oil in a saucepan.
2 Peel and slice the onion and garlic and fry gently for 2–3 minutes.
3 Drain the beans and add them to the saucepan with the tomatoes and tomato purée (paste) or sauce.
4 Heat through, then add the pasta and chopped parsley or dried herbs.
5 Simmer gently for 7–8 minutes, until the pasta is cooked.
6 Eat with crusty bread and a green salad.

7 ▪ red kidney beans

These kidney-shaped, dark red-brown beans are excellent in salads and stews – most people recognise them as a main ingredient of chilli con carne. They have a firm texture and a slightly sweet flavour. The canned ones are now readily available in all supermarkets. Dried kidney beans need to be soaked for 3–4 hours and then cooked for 1½–2 hours.

frankfurters and beans

Servings: 1
Time to prepare: 15 minutes

Ingredients	Metric	Imperial	American
tin red kidney beans	200g	7oz	7oz
tin tomatoes	200g	7oz	7oz
oil	1 tbsp	1 tbsp	1 tbsp
small onion	1	1	1
clove garlic	1	1	1
frankfurters	2	2	2
mixed herbs	1 tsp	1 tsp	1 tsp
salt and pepper			

Equipment
Saucepan, sieve, chopping board, knife

Cooking method
Top of stove

1 Heat the oil in a saucepan.
2 Peel and slice the onion and garlic and fry gently for 2–3 minutes.
3 Empty the red kidney beans into the sieve and rinse thoroughly; then add to the saucepan.

4 Add the tomatoes, chopped frankfurters and herbs.
5 Season with salt and pepper.
6 Heat through for about 10 minutes.
7 Eat with crusty bread.

chilli beans

Servings: 1
Time to prepare: 15 minutes

Ingredients	Metric	Imperial	American
tin red kidney beans (or 100g/4oz dried, cooked)	200g	7oz	7oz
oil	1 tbsp	1 tbsp	1 tbsp
small red or green (bell) pepper, chopped	1	1	1
small onion, finely chopped	1	1	1
chilli powder	1/2 tsp	1/2 tsp	1/2 tsp
dried mixed herbs	1/2 tsp	1/2 tsp	1/2 tsp
tomato purée (paste)	1 tsp	1 tsp	1 tsp
salt and pepper			

Equipment
Saucepan, sieve, chopping board, knife

Cooking method
Top of stove

1 Heat the oil in a saucepan and gently fry the chopped pepper and onion for 5 minutes.
2 Empty the red kidney beans into the sieve and rinse thoroughly; then add to the saucepan.
3 Add the rest of the ingredients and continue cooking for another 10 minutes.

chilli con carne

Servings: 2
Time to prepare: 1 hour

These quantities are enough for two meals, served with rice or a jacket potato. This is a good dish to make when you have hungry friends to feed – just multiply the quantities accordingly. If you plan to save the second portion to eat the following day, it must be recooked right through, not just warmed. Always keep any leftovers in the refrigerator overnight.

Ingredients	Metric	Imperial	American
tin red kidney beans (or 100g/4oz dried, cooked)	200g	7oz	7oz
tin tomatoes	200g	7oz	7oz
oil	1 tbsp	1 tbsp	1 tbsp
onion	1	1	1
clove of garlic	1	1	1
green (bell) pepper	1/2	1/2	1/2
minced (ground) meat	225g	8oz	1 cup
chilli powder (more if you like it hot!)	1 tsp	1 tsp	1 tsp
salt and pepper			

Equipment
Saucepan, sieve, chopping board, knife

Cooking method
Top of stove

1 Heat the oil in a saucepan.
2 Peel and slice the onion and garlic, chop the green pepper, and fry gently for 2–3 minutes.
3 Add the meat and fry them until browned.
4 Add the tomatoes and chilli powder.
5 Season with salt and pepper.

6 Bring to the boil and simmer for 30 minutes.
7 Drain the red kidney beans through the sieve, rinse well and add to the saucepan.
8 Cook for a further 30 minutes.

8 ▪ lentils

These come in different sizes and colours – red, yellow, green and brown. The most useful ones are the red and yellow, which cook down to a smooth purée. They are used a great deal in Indian cooking to make rich, mildly spiced dishes to go with meat and vegetable curries. These are called *dhals*. Lentils are also good for thick winter soups.

dhal

Servings: 2
Time to prepare: 30 minutes

Ingredients	Metric	Imperial	American
red lentils	$1/2$ cup	$1/2$ cup	$1/2$ cup
water	1 cup	1 cup	1 cup
small onion, finely chopped	1	1	1
clove of garlic, crushed	1	1	1
pinch of ground ginger			
pinch of turmeric			

Equipment
Saucepan, chopping board, knife

Cooking method
Top of stove

1 Put all the ingredients into a saucepan and bring to the boil.

2 Reduce the heat and simmer for 30 minutes, or until the lentils are soft and have absorbed all the water. (Check occasionally to make sure it does not become too dry – add a little extra water if necessary.)

lentil soup

Servings: 1
Time to prepare: 25 minutes

Ingredients	Metric	Imperial	American
red lentils	*1 tbsp*	*1 tbsp*	*1 tbsp*
small onion, finely chopped	*1*	*1*	*1*
small carrot, grated	*1*	*1*	*1*
stick celery, chopped thinly	*1*	*1*	*1*
oil	*1 tbsp*	*1 tbsp*	*1 tbsp*
water	*300ml*	*1/2 pt*	*1 1/4 cups*
tomato purée (paste)	*1 tsp*	*1 tsp*	*1 tsp*
salt and pepper			

Equipment
Saucepan, grater, chopping board, knife

Cooking method
Top of stove

1 Heat the oil in a saucepan and gently cook the onion, carrot and celery for 5 minutes.
2 Add the lentils and cook for a further 1 minute.
3 Add the water and tomato purée (paste).
4 Bring to the boil, cover with a lid, and simmer for 20 minutes.
5 Season with salt and pepper.

lentil curry

Servings: 1
Time to prepare: 25 minutes

Ingredients	Metric	Imperial	American
red lentils	$^1/_2$ cup	$^1/_2$ cup	$^1/_2$ cup
small onion, thinly sliced	1	1	1
oil	1 tbsp	1 tbsp	1 tbsp
curry powder	1 tsp	1 tsp	1 tsp
tomato purée (paste)	1 tbsp	1 tbsp	1 tbsp
small potato, diced	1	1	1
carrot, diced	1	1	1
button mushrooms, chopped	$^1/_2$ cup	$^1/_2$ cup	$^1/_2$ cup
peas, frozen or tinned	$^1/_2$ cup	$^1/_2$ cup	$^1/_2$ cup

Equipment
Saucepan, chopping board, knife

Cooking method
Top of stove

1 Heat the oil in a saucepan.
2 Gently fry the onions and lentils for 5 minutes.
3 Add just enough water to cover the lentils.
4 Continue cooking for a further 10–15 minutes until the water is absorbed.
5 Add the curry powder and tomato purée (paste) and stir well.
6 Add the vegetables and a little more water.
7 Cover and simmer for another 10–15 minutes, until the vegetables are cooked.
8 Serve with rice.

bread

Bread will remain fresh for several days if you keep it in a covered bread bin or loosely wrapped in a plastic bag so that the air can circulate. Alternatively, keep it – wrapped – in the fridge. It takes quite a long time for one person to get through a whole loaf, so if you have access to a freezer you could freeze part of the loaf for future consumption. If it is a sliced loaf, the slices can be removed individually – and you can toast them from frozen if you forget to defrost in time.

Many people prefer wholemeal bread these days because it contains all the natural nutrients, and more fibre than white bread. However, white bread usually has nutrients added by the baker – check the wrapping to make sure. Wheatmeal bread is often made from white flour which has been coloured brown.

If you have some bread that has gone a little stale, you could use it up in a bread pudding (see below). But once it has green specks or mould round the edges – throw it out or feed it to the birds.

bread and butter pudding

Servings: 2
Time to prepare: 1 hour (including standing time)

This is just as delicious cold, so make enough for two helpings. You can use fat-free margarine instead of butter.

Ingredients	Metric	Imperial	American
slices of buttered bread (white or brown)	4	4	4
currants or sultanas (golden raisins)	2 tbsp	2 tbsp	2 tbsp
sugar	1 tbsp	1 tbsp	1 tbsp
milk	450ml	³/₄ pt	2 cups
eggs	2	2	2
ground nutmeg	¹/₂ tsp	¹/₂ tsp	¹/₂ tsp

Equipment
Ovenproof dish, saucepan, basin, knife

Cooking method
Top of stove, and oven

1 Grease an ovenproof dish.
2 Cut the bread and butter into 2.5cm/1in squares and arrange them in the dish, buttered side up.
3 Sprinkle with the fruit and sugar.
4 Warm the milk in a saucepan.
5 Break the eggs into a basin and whisk thoroughly with a fork.
6 Pour the warm milk onto the eggs, stirring all the time.
7 Pour the egg and milk mixture over the bread.
8 Sprinkle the ground nutmeg on top.
9 Leave to stand for ¹/₂ hour so that the bread absorbs the milk.
10 Heat the oven to 350°F/180°C Gas Mark 4.
11 Bake in the centre of the oven for 30 minutes until lightly brown.

1 ▪ sandwiches and rolls

There will always be times when you want a packed lunch. Put sandwiches and rolls in a plastic bag or clingfilm (plastic wrap) to keep them fresh – wrapped like this they will remain fresh overnight in the fridge, so you save time making them in the morning. A plastic container to carry them in will stop them getting squashed.

Perhaps for economy's sake you need to make sandwiches every day – in which case here are a few tips and ideas to stop them becoming boring. For a start you could use different types of bread – all supermarkets have a good selection of white, brown, granary, crusty rolls, baps, and French bread. Always spread with margarine or butter first because this stops the bread going soggy and holds the filling in place. Here are some suggested fillings:

Bacon: Make while the bacon is still warm so that the fat sinks into the bread.
Banana: Sliced, on its own or with peanut butter.
Beef: Sliced very thinly, with mustard or horseradish sauce.
Cheese: Sliced or grated, with chutney, lettuce and mayonnaise, tomato, cucumber, onion or vegetable extract (e.g. Marmite).
Cottage cheese: With pineapple, cucumber or chopped dates.
Chicken: Either left over from a roast, or chicken roll slices, with salad or cranberry jelly.
Cream cheese: With sliced celery and/or walnuts.
Egg: Hardboiled, mashed with mayonnaise or tomato ketchup, or with cress.
Ham: With mustard, tomato, or lettuce.
Sardine: Mashed, with cucumber or tomato ketchup.
Tuna fish: Mashed with mayonnaise, with cucumber or lettuce.

● *Electric sandwich toasters are great for making quick hot snacks – but you can always toast your sandwiches under the grill (broiler).*

2 ▪ toast

This is one of the most obvious things to do with a slice of bread, and there are all kinds of things that go well on top – perhaps some that you haven't even thought of:

Anchovies: Mash some anchovies with a little tomato purée (paste) and spread on thick toast.

Cinnamon: Toast the bread on one side; sprinkle sugar and cinnamon on the untoasted side; put under the grill (broiler) until the sugar and cinnamon melt into each other.

Garlic mushrooms: Fry the mushrooms with a clove of garlic (crushed) in a little butter or oil, then pile on top of the ready-made toast.

Sardines: Mash with a fork, add a spoonful of tomato ketchup, or a few drops of Worcestershire sauce, lemon juice or vinegar, then spread on the toast. (For cheese on toast, see the Cheese Section; see also the Bean Section).

3 ▪ fried bread

This tastes best if you cook it in the frying pan (skillet) in the fat left from frying bacon. Fry in hot fat over a moderate heat for 1–2 minutes on each side, until it is golden brown and crisp.

A variation, called *pain perdu*, is to dip the slices of bread in egg beaten up with a little milk before you fry them.

fried cheese sandwiches

Servings: 1
Time to prepare: 10 minutes

Ingredients	Metric	Imperial	American
slices of bread	2	2	2
a knob of butter or margarine			
slices of cheese			
cooking oil	1 tbsp	1 tbsp	1 tbsp

Equipment
Frying pan (skillet), fish slice (pancake turner)

Cooking method
Top of stove

1 Butter the slices of bread and make two sandwiches with the cheese.
2 Heat the oil in a frying pan (skillet).
3 Put the sandwiches into the pan and fry for a few minutes on each side, until the bread is golden and crisp and the cheese is beginning to melt.
4 Lift out and drain on kitchen paper.
5 Eat at once while they are still hot.

4 ▪ French bread

Most supermarkets now sell French loaves. They seem to keep a bit better than the real French ones, but, nevertheless, they lose their appeal when no longer fresh. A loaf or part of one left over from the day before can be perked up by putting it in a moderately hot oven for a few minutes – or slice it and toast under the grill (broiler).

Eat French bread smothered in jam for breakfast, or with cheese or pâté for lunch – or try one of the ideas below.

French bread pizza

Servings: 1
Time to prepare: 10 minutes

You can use whatever toppings you like for this – you will find some more ideas in the pizza section.

Ingredients	Metric	Imperial	American
French loaf	$^1/_2$	$^1/_2$	$^1/_2$
tomato, sliced	1	1	1
slices of ham	2	2	2
slices of Cheddar cheese	4	4	4

Equipment
Chopping board, knife

Cooking method
Grill (broiler)

1 Split the loaf in half lengthways.
2 Arrange slices of tomato, ham and cheese on both halves.
3 Cook under a hot grill (broiler) until the cheese is brown and bubbling.

garlic bread

Servings: 1
Time to prepare: 20 minutes

Ingredients	Metric	Imperial	American
French loaf	$^1/_2$	$^1/_2$	$^1/_2$
clove of garlic, crushed (or $^1/_2$ tsp garlic powder or paste)	1	1	1
butter (or margarine)	50g	2oz	$^1/_4$ cup

Equipment
Chopping board, sharp knife, aluminium foil

Cooking method
Oven

1 Preheat the oven to 400°F/200°C Gas Mark 7.
2 Cut the loaf into 2.5cm/1in slices, but without going right the way through.
3 Cream the butter and garlic together.
4 Spread the mixture on both sides of the cut slices.
5 Wrap the loaf loosely in aluminium foil.
6 Heat in the oven for 5–10 minutes, until hot and crisp.

5 ▪ pitta bread

Most supermarkets now sell this flat, oblong-shaped unleavened bread. You buy them in packets of four, six or eight. Warm the pitta first under the grill (broiler), then tear off pieces to scoop up bolognese sauce, or humus. Alternatively, you can open the bread up to form a pocket and fill it with one of the following:

Salad: Shredded lettuce, sliced tomatoes and cucumber, grated cheese or ham – or whatever you fancy. Add some salad dressing or mayonnaise.
Minced meat: Fry an onion and some lean minced (ground) meat together; spoon into the pitta and add shredded lettuce and/or sliced tomato.
Chilli: Fry an onion and half a green (bell) pepper, add a tablespoon of red kidney beans and a pinch of chilli powder.

● *Pitta Pizzas can be made in the same way as French Bread Pizzas*

breakfast

Everyone swears they don't have time for it – but breakfast need not be complicated and you will function better with something inside you. It also lessens the need for mid-morning snacks. A glass of orange juice and toast, or a bowl of cereal with milk, is fine, but if you want something a bit more substantial, an egg is ideal (see the section on Eggs for ways of cooking them).

traditional English breakfast

You might fancy this occasionally – perhaps when you have got up late so that it is a combination of breakfast and lunch.

Servings: 1
Time to prepare: 12–15 minutes

Ingredients	Metric	Imperial	American
rashers (slices) of bacon (streaky, collar or back)	*1–2*	*1–2*	*1–2*
eggs	*1–2*	*1–2*	*1–2*
tomato, halved	*1*	*1*	*1*
mushrooms	*2–3*	*2–3*	*2–3*
slice of bread	*1*	*1*	*1*
oil for frying			

Equipment
Frying pan (skillet), fish slice (pancake turner)

Cooking method
Top of stove

1 Put a plate under the grill (broiler) to warm.
2 Heat 1 tablespoon oil in a large frying pan (skillet) over a medium heat.
3 Put the bacon in the pan and fry for 2–3 minutes on each side.
4 Push the bacon to one side of the pan and add the halved tomatoes and the mushrooms. Fry them for about 3 minutes, turning to cook both sides.
5 Push the tomato and mushrooms to the side to make room for the egg(s).
6 Break the egg(s) into a cup and slide into hot fat.
7 Lower the heat a little and cook until the white part of the egg is set.
8 Using a fish slice (pancake turner), lift everything out of the frying pan onto a warmed plate.
9 Turn up the heat and add a little more oil.
10 When the oil is hot, fry the slice of bread until it is golden and crisp on both sides.
11 Remove from the pan and put on the plate with the rest of the breakfast.

muesli

Muesli is more filling than most cereals, and it works out cheaper if you make your own. Mix together equal amounts of rolled oats and wheatflakes, and then add some or all of the following: raisins, currants, dates, dried banana, nuts. Store your muesli in a covered plastic container.

At breakfast-time, put 2 or 3 tablespoons of your muesli mixture into a bowl and add milk. You could also add some fresh fruit, or use yoghurt instead of milk.

porridge

Recently it has been suggested that oats are particularly good for you because they help reduce the level of cholesterol in the blood. Porridge makes a delicious warming start to the day. If you buy the instant variety all you have to do is stir in some hot milk. Rolled oats are cheaper, and the resulting porridge has more bulk.

Put 1 cup of porridge oats and 2–2$\frac{1}{2}$ cups of water, or part milk and part water, into a small saucepan. Add a pinch of salt. Bring to the boil and then simmer for 3–5 minutes, stirring occasionally to stop it sticking. If you prefer your porridge sweet, add sugar or golden syrup before you eat it.

the Cs

casseroles

A casserole is a mixture of meat and vegetables and a small amount of liquid cooked together in the oven, in a dish that has a close-fitting lid. The secret of a good casserole is slow cooking at a low heat – the slower the better to allow the flavours to mix together. Any heatproof dish with a lid will do – Pyrex, earthenware, or enamelled cast iron (see also the section on Slow Cooking). It's a good idea to cook enough for two meals. Second time round it will taste even better because the flavours will have had more time to blend well – you can heat up the second portion in a saucepan if you don't want to put the oven on again.

The really easy way to do a casserole is to buy one of the many tins or packets of commercially-prepared sauces that are available. With hardly any effort at all you can make *coq au vin*, *bœuf bourguignon* and a whole range of other dishes – but this will add to the cost of your meal, and it doesn't require much more effort to make your own sauce. It will certainly taste better.

The following are suitable to use in casseroles: the cheaper, tougher cuts of meat are ideal.

1 ▪ meat

Beef: Leg or shin, or whatever is described as stewing, braising, chuck, or 'for stews and casseroles'. Remove any fat and cut into cubes.
Chicken: Leg or breast joints.
Lamb: Chump or 'best end' (rib or loin) chops – make sure all the fat is cut off.
Liver: Lamb's liver; the others have a rather strong taste. Cut any pipe from the liver and slice into thin strips.
Pork: Belly pork (fresh pork sides), or shoulder (blade or spare rib) chops. Remove surplus fat and cut into cubes.

2 ▪ vegetables

Carrots: Peel or scrape and slice into rings.
Celery: Wash well and slice into small pieces.
Courgettes (zucchini): Trim off the ends, wash and slice into rings.
Leeks: Wash well and slice into rings.
Mushrooms: Small button ones are best. Use whole, without peeling. Wash them well.
Onions: Peel and slice into rings.
Parsnips: Peel and slice.
Peas: Fresh, frozen or tinned. If you use tinned ones, drain off the juice.
Peppers (bell): Red, green or yellow. Remove the top and the seeds and cut into thin strips.

Potatoes: Peel and cut into halves or quarters. Small new ones can be used whole.

Sweetcorn (corn kernels): Frozen or tinned. If you use tinned, drain off the juice.

Tomatoes: Fresh or tinned. Tinned ones provide more liquid, so you don't need as much stock.

Turnips: Peel and slice.

3 ▪ herbs and flavourings

Garlic: 1 clove, crushed, improves the flavour of 'Mediterranean-type' dishes with peppers and tomatoes.

Herbs: A dessertspoon of fresh, chopped herbs – parsley, thyme, majoram, rosemary, basil, etc. – or $1/2$ teaspoon dried mixed herbs. Or a 'bouquet garni' – a sprig each of parsley and thyme, plus a bayleaf, tied together with string and put into the casserole while it cooks. It is removed before serving.

Stock (bouillon) cubes: Beef, chicken, ham or vegetable – you simply dissolve one in hot water.

Soup: Packet soups, or tinned condensed soups, used undiluted, make excellent sauces for casseroles.

Tomato purée (paste): A couple of teaspoons added to the stock enriches the flavour.

Wine or cider: A tablespoon or so added to the stock improves the flavour.

Worcestershire sauce: A couple of dashes adds a bit of spice to beef casseroles.

4 ▪ basic method for casserole dishes

1 It is best to seal meat before putting it into the casserole dish, because this retains the flavour of the juices. Melt some fat in a frying pan (skillet), and when it is really hot add the cut-up meat. Fry

quickly, stirring all the time, until it is brown on all sides. Put the meat into the casserole dish.

2 Wash or peel the vegetables that you are using. Chop into pieces and add to the casserole dish.

3 Make stock by dissolving a stock (bouillon) cube in hot water.

4 Add whatever herbs or flavourings you are using to the stock. Season with salt and pepper and pour over the meat and vegetables.

5 Cover with a closely-fitting lid, or with foil.

6 Cook slowly in a low or moderate oven, for $1\frac{1}{2}$–$2\frac{1}{2}$ hours – or in a slow cooker – until the meat is well cooked and tender.

7 If you are reheating the second portion in the oven, allow 30–40 minutes at 350°F/180°C Gas Mark 4. If reheating in a saucepan, make sure you bring it to boiling point, and then simmer for 20 minutes.

chicken casserole

Servings: 2
Time to prepare: 1 hour 45 minutes

Scalloped potatoes go really well with this chicken dish (see the Potato section).

Ingredients	Metric	Imperial	American
chicken joints	2	2	2
oil	1 tbsp	1 tbsp	1 tbsp
small packet of frozen mixed vegetables	1	1	1
tin condensed cream of chicken soup (undiluted)	1	1	1
salt and pepper			
clove of garlic, crushed (optional)	1	1	1

Equipment
Ovenproof dish with lid, frying pan (skillet)

Cooking method
Oven

1 Heat the oven to 375°F/190°C Gas Mark 5.
2 Fry the chicken joints in the oil, turning them to make sure they are browned all over.
3 Put the joints into an ovenproof dish.
4 Add the mixed vegetables.
5 Pour over the undiluted soup.
7 Add the garlic if you are using it.
8 Cover with a lid and cook for 1½ hours, or until the chicken is tender.

lamb casserole

Servings: 2
Time to prepare: 1 hour 45 minutes

Ingredients	Metric	Imperial	American
lamb chops	2–4	2–4	2–4
oil	1 tbsp	1 tbsp	1 tbsp
potatoes, peeled and sliced thickly	2–3	2–3	2–3
packet spring vegetable soup mix	1	1	1
salt and pepper			

Equipment
Ovenproof dish with lid, frying pan (skillet)

Cooking method
Oven

1 Heat the oven to 375°F/190°C Gas Mark 5.
2 Fry the lamb chops in the oil for a couple of minutes to seal in the juices, then put into an ovenproof dish.
3 Arrange the potato on top.

4 To the soup mix, add half the amount of water required on the packet.
5 Pour over the meat and potatoes.
6 Season with salt and pepper.
7 Cover with a lid and cook for 1¹/₂ hours or until the lamb is tender.
8 Remove the lid half an hour before the end of cooking time to brown the potatoes.

pork casserole

Servings: 2
Time to prepare: 2¹/₂ hours

Ingredients	Metric	Imperial	American
lean pork, boned	350g	12oz	12oz
oil	1 tbsp	1 tbsp	1 tbsp
onion, peeled and sliced	1	1	1
cooking (tart) apple, peeled and sliced	1	1	1
dried mixed herbs	¹/₂ tsp	¹/₂ tsp	¹/₂ tsp
salt and pepper			

Equipment
Ovenproof dish with lid, chopping board, sharp knife, frying pan (skillet)

Cooking method
Oven

1 Heat the oven to 325°F/170°C Gas Mark 3.
2 Cut the pork into 1cm/¹/₂in cubes and fry for a couple of minutes in the oil to seal in the juices.
3 Put half the meat into the bottom of an ovenproof dish.

4 Arrange the sliced onion and apple on top, and sprinkle with herbs.
5 Add the remaining pork cubes.
6 Season with salt and pepper.
7 Cover with a lid and cook in the oven for 2–2½ hours, until the pork is tender.

beef in beer

Servings: 2
Time to prepare: 1 hour 45 minutes

Ingredients	Metric	Imperial	American
braising steak	*225g*	*8oz*	*8oz*
flour	*1 tbsp*	*1 tbsp*	*1 tbsp*
salt and pepper			
oil	*1 tbsp*	*1 tbsp*	*1 tbsp*
onion, peeled and sliced	*1*	*1*	*1*
carrot, peeled and sliced	*1*	*1*	*1*
mushrooms, sliced	*4–5*	*4–5*	*4–5*
beer	*3 tbsp*	*3 tbsp*	*3 tbsp*
tomato purée (paste)	*1 tsp*	*1 tsp*	*1 tsp*
mixed herbs	*½ tsp*	*½ tsp*	*½ tsp*

Equipment
Frying pan (skillet), ovenproof dish with lid, chopping board, sharp knife, fish slice (pancake turner)

Cooking method
Oven

1 Preheat the oven to 350°F/180°C Gas Mark 4.
2 Cut the meat into 1cm/½in cubes.
3 Put the flour onto a plate and add a sprinkling of salt and pepper.

4 Toss the meat cubes in this until they are all coated with seasoned flour.

5 Heat the oil in a frying pan (skillet) and cook all the vegetables gently for 2 minutes.

6 With a fish slice (pancake turner) or slotted spoon transfer the vegetables to an ovenproof dish.

7 Put the meat into the frying pan (skillet) and cook for 3–4 minutes, stirring all the time until the meat is browned on all sides.

8 Transfer to the ovenproof dish.

9 Mix the tomato purée (paste) with the beer and pour over the meat and vegetables.

10 Sprinkle on the herbs, and some salt and pepper.

11 Cover with a lid and cook in the oven for $1\frac{1}{2}$–2 hours, until the beef is tender.

cheese

Cheese is a very adaptable food – you can use it in cooking, either as a main ingredient, for flavouring sauces or as a topping; and it is excellent for eating as a quick snack. Because it is so rich in protein, cheese is an excellent substitute for meat in vegetarian dishes. It is also a good source of calcium and vitamin A. But slimmers beware – it is also high in fat.

In the supermarket you will find that cheese is sold prepacked or loose. It is cheaper to buy pieces of cheese cut from a whole cheese, and it also tastes better. But don't buy too much – once cheese is cut it deteriorates, so limit yourself to just enough for two or three days. Cheese should be kept in the refrigerator wrapped in clingfilm (plastic wrap) or foil. However, the coldness lessens the flavour, so take it out at least half an hour before you want to eat it.

Welsh rarebit

Servings: 2
Time to prepare: 10 minutes

Ingredients	Metric	Imperial	American
slices of bread	2	2	2
butter or margarine	1 tbsp	1 tbsp	1 tbsp
grated Caerphilly cheese	50g	2oz	1/2 cup
salt and pepper			
mustard	1/4 tsp	1/4 tsp	1/4 tsp
milk	1	1	1

Equipment
Small saucepan, grater

Cooking method
Grill (broiler)

1 Toast the bread under the grill (broiler).
2 Butter the toast, using half the butter, and keep hot.
3 Melt the rest of the butter in a small saucepan.
4 Remove from the heat and add the grated cheese, a little salt and pepper, and the mustard.
5 Stir in enough milk to make a stiff paste.
6 Spread the cheese paste onto the toast.
7 Grill (broil) gently until golden brown.

cheese on toast

Servings: 1
Time to prepare: 10 minutes

Ingredients	Metric	Imperial	American
slices of bread	2	2	2
butter or margarine			
Cheddar cheese	50g	2oz	2oz

Equipment
Knife

Cooking method
Grill (broiler)

1 Slice the cheese thinly.
2 Toast the bread under the grill (broiler).
3 Turn over and spread the untoasted side with butter.
4 Arrange the cheese evenly on top.
5 Put back under the grill and cook until the cheese is golden brown and bubbling.

● *You can add other things to this basic recipe to make a more substantial snack – for example a slice of ham underneath the cheese, or a sliced tomato. Grilled (broiled) bacon and a fried or poached egg can be put on top.*

cauliflower cheese

Servings: 1
Time to prepare: 20–25 minutes.

The easiest way to make this dish is to use a packet of cheese sauce mix – make it up according to the instructions. Or you can just cover the cauliflower with grated cheese and then grill (broil) it. But if you want to make your own sauce, here's how.

Ingredients	Metric	Imperial	American
cauliflower	1/2	1/2	1/2
butter or margarine	1 tsp	1 tsp	1 tsp
flour	2 tsp	2 tsp	2 tsp
milk	1 cup	1 cup	1 cup
salt and pepper			
mustard	1/2 tsp	1/2 tsp	1/2 tsp
mature Cheddar cheese, grated	50g	2oz	1/2 cup

Equipment
Saucepan, sieve, grater, fireproof dish

Cooking method
Top of stove, then grill (broiler)

1 Trim the cauliflower stalk and divide the cauliflower into florets.
2 Wash the florets thoroughly.
3 Cook the cauliflower in a saucepan of boiling, salted water for 15 minutes.
4 Drain into a sieve, then arrange the cooked florets in a fireproof dish.
5 Rinse out the saucepan and dry it.
6 Put the butter into the saucepan and heat gently until it has just melted – do not allow it to go brown.
7 Stir in the flour and cook gently for 1 minute.
8 Remove the pan from the heat and very gradually stir in the milk. (This is the tricky bit – if you don't stir thoroughly you will get horrible lumps instead of a smooth sauce!)
9 Return the pan to the heat and – still stirring – bring the sauce to the boil.
10 The sauce will now have thickened. Remove it from the heat and stir in half the grated cheese and the mustard.
11 Season with salt and pepper.
12 Pour the cheese sauce over the cauliflower and sprinkle the rest of the cheese on top.
13 Put under a hot grill (broiler) for a few minutes until the top is browned.

cheese and potato pie

Servings: 1
Time to prepare: 30 minutes

If you are using up left-over boiled potatoes this dish will take only 10 minutes to prepare.

Ingredients	Metric	Imperial	American
large potatoes	*2*	*2*	*2*
a knob of margarine or butter			
milk	*1 tbsp*	*1 tbsp*	*1 tbsp*
salt and pepper			
grated Cheddar cheese	*50g*	*2oz*	*½ cup*
tomato	*1*	*1*	*1*

Equipment
Saucepan, sieve, grater, fireproof dish (e.g. Pyrex), sharp knife

Cooking method
Top of stove, then grill (broiler)

1 Peel the potatoes and cut into even-sized pieces.
2 Put potatoes into a saucepan and cover with cold water; add ½ teaspoon salt.
3 Put the lid on the pan and bring the water to boiling point.
4 Reduce the heat and simmer gently until the potatoes are soft (15–20 minutes).
5 Drain the potatoes into a sieve and then return them to the saucepan.
6 Mash the potatoes with a fork.
7 Add the margarine or butter, milk, and a little salt and pepper.
8 Beat until the potatoes are creamy, then add half the grated cheese.

9 Spoon the mashed potato into a fireproof dish and sprinkle on the rest of the cheese.
10 Slice the tomato thinly and arrange on top as a garnish.
11 Put under a hot grill (broiler) until the top is golden brown.

cheesy rice

Servings: 1
Time to prepare: 10 minutes

This is a good way of using up left-over cooked rice.

Ingredients	Metric	Imperial	American
small onion	1	1	1
slices of bacon	2	2	2
oil	1 tbsp	1 tbsp	1 tbsp
cooked rice	1 cup	1 cup	1 cup
grated Gruyère (or Cheddar) cheese	2 tbsp	2 tbsp	2 tbsp
salt and pepper			

Equipment
Frying pan (skillet), sharp knife, chopping board

Cooking method
Top of stove

1 Peel and chop the onion, and cut the bacon into small pieces.
2 Heat the oil in a frying pan (skillet) and gently cook the onion and bacon for 5 minutes.
3 Add the rice and cheese, and season with salt and pepper.
4 Continue cooking, stirring all the time, until everything is well mixed and heated through.

chicken

Chicken is very good value for money and contains little fat. If you buy it frozen you must defrost it completely before cooking. You can speed this up by holding the chicken joint under cold running water, or putting it in a bowl of cold water. Never use hot water because germs thrive in warm conditions and chicken is particularly prone to nasty bacteria. For the same reason, chicken must always be thoroughly cooked – when you pierce it with a fork the juices should run clear, not pink.

1 ▪ chicken joints

You will have a choice of breast, leg or drumsticks. Breast needs less cooking. Fresh chicken tastes better and is more tender than frozen, but also costs more – you get what you pay for!

fried chicken

Servings: 1
Time to prepare: 25 minutes

Ingredients	Metric	Imperial	American
chicken joint, breast or leg	*1*	*1*	*1*
oil (or a knob of butter)	*1 tbsp*	*1 tbsp*	*1 tbsp*

Equipment
Frying pan (skillet)

Cooking method
Top of stove

1 Defrost the chicken thoroughly if it is frozen.

2 Heat the oil or butter in a frying pan (skillet) over a moderate heat.

3 Fry the chicken for about 20 minutes, turning it from time to time so that it is browned on all sides.

fried chicken with tomato sauce

Servings: 1
Time to prepare: 1 hour

Ingredients	Metric	Imperial	American
joint of chicken	1	1	1
flour	1 tbsp	1 tbsp	1 tbsp
salt and pepper			
oil	1 tbsp	1 tbsp	1 tbsp
small onion, peeled and chopped	1	1	1
tomato sauce	2 tbsp	2 tbsp	2 tbsp
water	2 tbsp	2 tbsp	2 tbsp
vinegar	1 tbsp	1 tbsp	1 tbsp
brown sugar	1 tbsp	1 tbsp	1 tbsp
Worcestershire sauce	$^1/_2$ tsp	$^1/_2$ tsp	$^1/_2$ tsp

Equipment
Shallow dish or plate, frying pan (skillet) with lid, small basin

Cooking method
Top of stove

1 In a shallow dish or a plate mix the flour with a little salt and pepper.

2 Dip the chicken in the flour mixture so that it is coated on all sides.

3 Heat the oil in a frying pan (skillet) and add the chopped onion and the chicken.

4 Cook until the chicken is browned all over.
5 Mix the remaining ingredients together and pour over the chicken.
6 Cover with a lid or plate and cook for about 45 minutes, or until the chicken is tender.

chicken and rice

Servings: 1
Time to prepare: 45 minutes

Ingredients	Metric	Imperial	American
chicken joint	*1*	*1*	*1*
knob of butter (or margarine)			
small onion, finely chopped	*1*	*1*	*1*
carrot, thinly sliced	*1*	*1*	*1*
long-grain rice	*½ cup*	*½ cup*	*½ cup*
water			
dried mixed herbs	*½ tsp*	*½ tsp*	*½ tsp*
salt and pepper			

Equipment
Saucepan, chopping board, knife

Cooking method
Top of stove

1 Melt the butter in a saucepan and gently fry the onion and carrot.
2 Add the chicken joint and brown it on both sides.
3 Add the rice and enough water to cover everything.
4 Add the herbs and season with salt and pepper.
5 Bring to the boil, then reduce the heat, cover with a lid and simmer for 40 minutes.
6 Check occasionally to see if it is drying up – if so, add a little extra water.

2 ▪ boned chicken breasts

Chicken breast with the bone taken out costs more per pound, but remember that you are not paying for the bone. It is ideal if you are catering just for yourself because it is versatile, quick and easy to cook. All of these dishes go well with rice. (See also Stir-fry.)

lemon chicken

Servings: 1
Time to prepare: 5 minutes

Ingredients	Metric	Imperial	American
boned chicken breast	1	1	1
salt and pepper			
oil	1 tbsp	1 tbsp	1 tbsp
stock, made with a chicken stock (bouillon) cube	1 tbsp	1 tbsp	1 tbsp
lemon juice	1 tsp	1 tsp	1 tsp
soy sauce	1 tsp	1 tsp	1 tsp
spring onions (scallions), finely chopped	2	2	2

Equipment
Frying pan (skillet), chopping board, knife

Cooking method
Top of stove

1 Cut the chicken into thin strips and season it generously with salt and pepper.
2 Heat the oil in a frying pan and fry the chicken quickly, stirring all the time, until it is golden brown.
3 Add the stock, lemon juice and soy sauce.
4 Stir in the spring onions (scallions) and cook for 2–3 minutes.

Italian chicken

Servings: 1
Time to prepare: 20 minutes

Ingredients	Metric	Imperial	American
boned chicken breast	*1*	*1*	*1*
oil	*1 tbsp*	*1 tbsp*	*1 tbsp*
clove of garlic, crushed	*1*	*1*	*1*
small red (bell) pepper, finely chopped	*¹/₂*	*¹/₂*	*¹/₂*
small yellow (bell) pepper, finely chopped	*¹/₂*	*¹/₂*	*¹/₂*
tin chopped tomatoes	*200g*	*7oz*	*7oz*
mixed dried herbs	*¹/₂ tsp*	*¹/₂ tsp*	*¹/₂ tsp*
salt and pepper			

Equipment
Frying pan (skillet), chopping board, sharp knife

Cooking method
Top of stove

1 Heat the oil in a frying pan (skillet) and fry the crushed garlic for 1 minute.
2 Add the chicken breast and brown on both sides.
3 Add the peppers, tomatoes and herbs.
4 Season with salt and pepper.
5 Bring everything up to simmering point, then cook, without a lid, for 15 minutes.

chicken kebabs

Servings: 1
Time to prepare: 15 minutes

This will taste even better if you leave the chicken to marinate for at least half-an-hour before cooking.

Ingredients	Metric	Imperial	American
boned chicken breast	1	1	1
natural yoghurt	2 tbsp	2 tbsp	2 tbsp
honey	1 tbsp	1 tbsp	1 tbsp
clove of garlic, crushed	1	1	1
curry paste	1 tsp	1 tsp	1 tsp
yellow (bell) pepper, cut into cubes	$^1/_2$	$^1/_2$	$^1/_2$
button mushrooms	6	6	6

Equipment
Mixing bowl, chopping board, sharp knife, skewer(s)

Cooking method
Grill (broiler)

1 Cut the chicken into cubes.
2 Put into a bowl and add the yoghurt, honey, crushed garlic and curry paste.
3 Mix thoroughly and leave to stand for half-an-hour if you have time.
4 Pierce chicken onto the skewers alternately with yellow pepper and mushrooms.
5 Cook under a hot grill (broiler) for 15 minutes, turning frequently.

curry

The simplest way of making a curry is to buy a tin of ready-made sauce and then add meat or vegetables. It is not very much more trouble to make your own sauce using curry powder, and this is an excellent way of using up cooked meat left over from a Sunday roast. However, if you become a connoisseur of curries you will eventually find that curry powder on its own makes every spicy dish taste the same, and you may want to start building up a collection of spices so that you can produce the more subtle flavours.

Here are two simple curry sauces to start off with, followed by some others that use a variety of spices. It makes sense to cook at least enough for two servings because small amounts tend to dry up. The second portion will taste even better when it has been reheated, but make sure that it is brought to boiling point and then simmered for at least 15 minutes.

curry sauce for left-overs

Servings: 2
Time to prepare: 45 minutes

This sauce goes particularly well with beef and lamb.

Ingredients	Metric	Imperial	American
butter or margarine	*1 tbsp*	*1 tbsp*	*1 tbsp*
onions, peeled and sliced	*2*	*2*	*2*
curry powder	*2 tsp*	*2 tsp*	*2 tsp*
tin tomatoes	*200g*	*7oz*	*7oz*
left-over meat			

Equipment
Saucepan, chopping board, knife

Cooking method
Top of stove

1 Melt the butter in a saucepan over a moderate heat.
2 Add the sliced onion and cook gently until it is soft and transparent.
3 Sprinkle the curry powder over the onion and stir.
4 Allow to cook for another minute.
5 Stir in the tomatoes.
6 Bring to the boil, then reduce the heat so that the sauce simmers, and cover with a lid.
7 Simmer for 30 minutes, then add the left-over cooked meat and continue cooking for another 15 minutes.

sweet curry sauce

Servings: 2
Time to prepare: 45 minutes

This sweet curry sauce goes well with pork or eggs.

Ingredients	Metric	Imperial	American
butter or margarine	1 tbsp	1 tbsp	1 tbsp
onion, peeled and sliced	1	1	1
apple, peeled and sliced	1	1	1
flour	1 tbsp	1 tbsp	1 tbsp
curry powder	2 tsp	2 tsp	2 tsp
chicken stock (made by dissolving a stock (bouillon) cube in hot water)	300ml	$^{1}/_{2}$ pint	$1^{1}/_{4}$ cups
sultanas (golden raisins)	1 tbsp	1 tbsp	1 tsp
salt	$^{1}/_{2}$ tsp	$^{1}/_{2}$ tsp	$^{1}/_{2}$ tsp
lemon juice	1 tbsp	1 tbsp	1 tbsp
mango chutney	1 tbsp	1 tbsp	1 tbsp
left-over pork or hardboiled eggs			

Equipment
Saucepan, chopping board, knife

Cooking method
Top of stove

1 Melt the butter in a saucepan and gently fry the onion and apple until soft.
2 Stir in the flour and curry powder and cook for another minute.
3 Gradually add the stock, stirring all the time to stop lumps forming.
4 Add the sultanas (golden raisins).
5 Bring to the boil, reduce the heat, then cover with a lid.
6 Simmer for 30 minutes, then add the cooked pork or hardboiled eggs and simmer for another 15 minutes.
7 Stir in the lemon juice and mango chutney before serving.

side dishes to go with curries

Cucumber raita
This is a lovely cool accompaniment to a hot curry. Grate a 2.5cm/1in piece of cucumber and mix with 2 or 3 tablespoons of plain yoghurt. Sprinkle on a few cumin seeds or some cayenne pepper.

Tomato and onion
Chop a tomato and an onion into thin slices. Put them in a small bowl and add 1 tablespoon of wine vinegar and a little salt and pepper. Mix everything well and chill in the fridge for at least an hour.

beef curry

Servings: 2
Time to prepare: 1 hour

Ingredients	Metric	Imperial	American
oil	2 tbsp	2 tbsp	2 tbsp
small onion, peeled and finely chopped	1	1	1
piece of fresh ginger root, peeled and crushed	1cm	$^1/_2$ in	$^1/_2$ in
cloves of garlic, peeled and crushed	2	2	2
ground coriander	$^1/_2$ tsp	$^1/_2$ tsp	$^1/_2$ tsp
ground cumin	$^1/_2$ tsp	$^1/_2$ tsp	$^1/_2$ tsp
ground turmeric	$^1/_4$ tsp	$^1/_4$ tsp	$^1/_4$ tsp
chilli powder	$^1/_2$ tsp	$^1/_2$ tsp	$^1/_2$ tsp
salt	$^1/_2$ tsp	$^1/_2$ tsp	$^1/_2$ tsp
braising steak, cut into cubes	225g	8oz	8oz
tin tomatoes	200g	7oz	7oz

Equipment
Saucepan, chopping board, sharp knife

Cooking method
Top of stove

1 Heat the oil in a saucepan and gently fry the onion until it is transparent.
2 Add all the spices, salt and meat.
3 Mix well, then cover with a lid and cook over a gentle heat for 10 minutes.
4 Add the tomatoes and continue cooking for another 50 minutes, or until the meat is tender.

chicken korma

Servings: 2
Time to prepare: 50 minutes (plus 1–2 hours marinating time)

Ingredients	Metric	Imperial	American
chicken joints	2	2	2
yoghurt	2 tbsp	2 tbsp	2 tbsp
ground coriander	1/2 tsp	1/2 tsp	1/2 tsp
turmeric	1/2 tsp	1/2 tsp	1/2 tsp
ground cardamon	1/4 tsp	1/4 tsp	1/4 tsp
ground cumin	1/4 tsp	1/4 tsp	1/4 tsp
a pinch of ground ginger			
butter or margarine	1 tbsp	1 tbsp	1 tbsp
small onion, peeled and sliced	1	1	1
clove of garlic, peeled and crushed	1	1	1
water	1/2 cup	1/2 cup	1/2 cup
ground almonds	2 tsp	2 tsp	2 tsp

Equipment
Large saucepan or frying pan (skillet) with lid, mixing basin, sharp knife, fish slice (pancake turner) or slotted spoon

Cooking method
Top of stove

1 Remove the skin from the chicken joints and make incisions all over the flesh with a sharp knife.
2 Make a paste of the spices and a little of the yoghurt.
3 Spread this spicy mixture all over the chicken joints and leave them to marinate for at least an hour, preferably two.
4 When you are ready to cook melt the butter in a

large pan and gently cook the onion and garlic for 3 minutes.

5 Add the chicken joints and fry them until they are browned on both sides.
6 Add the water and bring to the boil.
7 Reduce the heat, cover with a lid and simmer for 30–40 minutes, until the chicken is tender.
8 Remove the chicken joints from the saucepan with a fish slice (pancake turner) or slotted spoon and put to one side.
9 Mix the rest of the yoghurt with the ground almonds and stir into the liquid in the saucepan.
10 Cook, stirring all the time, for 5 minutes.
11 Replace the chicken joints and heat through for 5 minutes.

vegetable curry

Servings: 1
Time to prepare: 30 minutes

This can be a side dish with a meat curry, or eaten on its own with rice.

Ingredients	Metric	Imperial	American
oil	1 tbsp	1 tbsp	1 tbsp
small onion, peeled and finely sliced	1	1	1
mixed vegetables, diced (e.g. potato, carrot, peas, beans, cauliflower)	1/2 cup	1/2 cup	1/2 cup
chilli powder	1/2 tsp	1/2 tsp	1/2 tsp
ground coriander	1 tsp	1 tsp	1 tsp
a pinch of ground turmeric			
a pinch of salt			
lemon juice	1 tbsp	1 tbsp	1 tbsp
water	1/2 cup	1/2 cup	1/2 cup

Equipment
Saucepan, chopping board, sharp knife

Cooking method
Top of stove

1 Heat the oil in a saucepan and gently fry the onion for 2–3 minutes until it is transparent.
2 Add the diced vegetables, and stir in the chilli powder, coriander, turmeric and salt.
3 Fry for 3 minutes.
4 Add the lemon juice and water (add less water if you want a dry curry).
5 Cover with a lid and simmer for 10–12 minutes, or until the vegetables are soft.

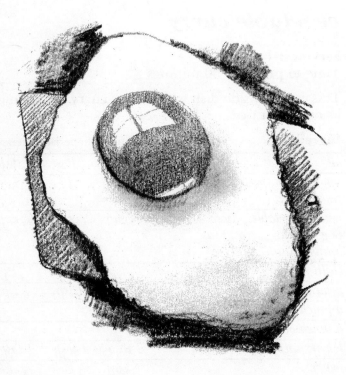

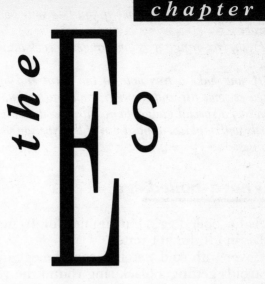

the E *s*

eggs

Eggs have a very high food value – they contain protein, as well as vitamins A, B, D, and iron and calcium in the yolk. It's unusual to come across a bad egg these days, but you can easily detect one by its smell. A fresh egg sinks in cold water, while a stale egg floats. Recently some people stopped eating eggs because salmonella poisoning was attributed to them. The official advice is to make sure they are properly cooked. There are several ways of cooking eggs.

1 ▪ boiled egg

1 Put an egg into a small saucepan and cover with cold water.
2 On a high heat, bring the water to the boil.
3 Reduce the heat and simmer the egg for 3 minutes.
4 Lift the egg out of the water with a spoon.

- *Increase the cooking time if you like your boiled egg a bit harder.*
- *Fresh, free-range eggs take longer to cook than supermarket ones.*
- *If you make a tiny hole in the blunt end of the egg this releases some air and the egg won't crack while cooking. You can buy a special gadget to do this, but it can be done just as easily with a plastic-topped pin of the type you use for pinning up posters.*

2 ▪ hard-boiled egg

1 As for boiled egg, but simmer for 10 minutes.
2 Drain off the hot water.
3 Cover with cold water to cool the egg quickly – this avoids getting a black ring round the yolk.
4 Remove the shell.
5 Eat the hard-boiled egg with salad, in mayonnaise as a starter, in a sandwich, in a cheese sauce (see p. 50) or in a curry sauce (see p. 60).

- *The best way to shell a hard-boiled egg is to tap it sharply on something hard to break the shell, then roll it between your hands until the shell is broken up all over. The shell then peels off easily.*

3 ▪ scrambled egg

1 Break the egg into a basin.
2 Add a pinch of salt and pepper and 1 tablespoon of milk.
3 Beat together with a fork.
4 Put a small saucepan on a low heat and add a knob of butter.
5 When the butter has melted add the beaten egg mixture.
6 Cook on low heat, stirring all the time with a

wooden spoon, for 2–3 minutes, until the egg is thick and creamy.

7 Serve on buttered bread or toast.

● *To break an egg, hold it over the basin and give it a sharp tap on the edge to break the shell. Put your thumbs into the crack and pull the shell apart so that the contents fall into the basin.*

4 ▪ poached egg

Poaching is a method of cooking eggs or fish in water. It is healthier than frying them in fat, and just as quick.

1 Put about 2.5cm (1in) water in a small frying pan (skillet) and bring to the boil.
2 Reduce the heat so that the water is simmering gently.
3 Break the egg into a cup and then slide it from the cup into the water, making sure you don't break the yolk.
4 Cook for 2–3 minutes, until the white of the egg is firm and set.
5 While the egg is cooking prepare a slice of bread or toast and butter.
6 Remove the egg from the water with a fish slice (pancake turner) or slotted spoon, so that it drains.
7 Place on the buttered bread or toast.

● *A dash of vinegar in the water helps the egg to keep its shape and to set more quickly.*

5 ▪ fried egg

1 Put 1 tablespoon cooking oil into a frying pan (skillet) and heat at a fairly high temperature.

2 When the oil is hot break the egg into the frying pan.

3 Lower the heat and cook until the egg white sets.

4 If you like your egg done on both sides, use a fish slice (pancake turner) to turn it over.

5 Remove from the frying pan with the fish slice (pancake turner).

• *If you are not very good at breaking eggs, it's probably a good idea to break it into a cup first, and then slip it into the frying pan.*

• *If you want egg and bacon, cook the bacon in the frying pan first, and then push it to one side to keep warm while you cook the egg in the remaining bacon fat.*

6 ▪ folded omelette

This is the type of omelette that you cook on one side first, then add a filling and fold one half over the other.

1 Break 2 eggs into a basin.

2 Add a pinch of salt and pepper and 1 tablespoon of cold water.

3 Beat together with a fork.

4 Heat your frying pan (skillet) to a fairly high temperature.

5 Add a small knob of butter (or margarine) and when it has melted – make sure that it does not burn and turn brown – pour in the eggs, swirling them over the bottom of the pan.

6 As the egg sets draw the cooked bits to the centre with a fish slice (pancake turner) or spatula, allowing the uncooked mixture to run to the sides. Tilt the pan as you work.

7 Before the omelette is completely set add your chosen filling and fold one half over the other.

8 Slide onto a warm plate.

Suggested fillings for folded omelettes
Add before you fold the omelette in half.

Cheese: Use 1 tablespoon finely grated Cheddar.
Onion: Sliced thinly and fried gently in butter.
Mushrooms: Fried gently in butter.
Tomato: 1 or 2 tomatoes, thinly sliced.
Ham: Cut into small cubes.

7 ▪ flat omelette

When you are really hungry the flat, pancake-like omelettes are the kind to go for. The quantities of additional ingredients can be much more generous than in the filling for a folded omelette. A Spanish omelette is a good example – but you can add whatever extra ingredients you like. With this type of omelette you cook the extra ingredients in the frying pan (skillet) first, then pour the beaten eggs over them.

Spanish omelette

Servings: 1
Time to prepare: 10 minutes (plus 20 mins if you haven't already cooked the potato)

Ingredients	Metric	Imperial	American
eggs	2–3	2–3	2–3
medium-sized potato, boiled	1	1	1
small onion	1	1	1
salt and pepper			
oil	1 tbsp	1 tbsp	1 tbsp

Equipment
Omelette pan, mixing basin, fork, sharp knife, chopping board, fish slice (pancake turner) or spatula

Cooking method
Top of stove

1 Break the eggs into a mixing basin.
2 Add a pinch of salt and pepper and beat with a fork.
3 Cut boiled potato into thin slices.
4 Peel and thinly slice the onion.
5 Put the omelette pan on fairly high heat and heat the oil.
6 Add the sliced onion and cook for 2–3 minutes until soft, but not brown.
7 Add the potato and continue cooking until both are beginning to brown.
8 Pour the beaten eggs into the omelette pan.
9 Stir gently with a fish slice (pancake turner) or spatula.
10 Turn the heat down and cook gently until the eggs are set but still a little moist.
11 Either turn the omelette over and cook the other side, or put the frying pan under a hot grill (broiler) to finish it.

● *This is a good way of using up left-over boiled potatoes from a previous meal. See p. 119 for boiled potatoes.*

the F s

fats and oils

We hear a lot about fat these days, and advice comes from all quarters to cut down on animal fats, which are thought to raise the level of cholesterol in our bodies and contribute to coronary heart disease. We all need a small amount of fat in our diet to provide certain vitamins and to make food tasty. But most of us eat far more fat than we need – and it's then that problems start.

Most foods contain a mixture of *saturated fats* and *unsaturated fats*. The difference between them is in their chemical make-up.

saturated fats

These are the dangerous animal fats, found in dairy products (cheese, butter, milk, cream), eggs and meat. They are also found in some vegetable oils such as coconut oil and palm oil, in hard margarines and cooking fats (such as lard), and hidden in cakes, biscuits (cookies), chocolate and puddings. It is a good idea to cut down on these saturated fats.

unsaturated fats

This group includes polyunsaturated fats and monounsaturated fats. They are found in vegetable oils such as sunflower, corn, soya, rapeseed and olive oils; in soft margarine labelled 'high in polyun-saturates'; in nuts; and in oily fish such as sardines, herring, mackerel, trout and pilchards. It is a good idea to eat these instead of saturated fats whenever possible.

ways to eat less fat

For the recipes in this book I have used unsaturated fats wherever possible. Here are some other ways of cutting down on the fat in your diet without making yourself thoroughly miserable in the process.

● Instead of butter, use a low-fat spread or a margarine labelled 'high in polyunsaturates'.

● Buy skimmed or semi-skimmed milk instead of whole milk. Both have just as much calcium and protein, but much less fat.

● Avoid cream – use low fat yoghurt or fromage frais instead.

● Look for a low-fat cheese, or choose cottage cheese sometimes instead.

● Buy lean meat, and eat less of it. In particular choose minced (ground) meat with the lowest fat content. Stir-frying is a particularly good way of cooking small amounts of lean meat.

● Chicken has less fat than red meat, and most of it is just under the skin. Remove the skin before cooking.

● Don't eat chips (French fries) – eat baked potatoes instead.

● If you cut down on fat, you also cut down calories. This is fine if you want to lose weight, but if you don't you can fill up on starchy foods that are high in fibre, such as wholemeal bread, cereals, rice, beans and pasta. There are plenty of recipe ideas in this book.

fat content of various foods

Food	grams per portion
butter	8
low fat spread	4
milk – full cream	22
– semi-skimmed	9
– skimmed	0.6
cream	14
low fat yoghurt	0.3
low fat fromage frais	0.3
chips (French fries) – thin cut	17
– thick cut	8
– oven	7
baked potato	0.1
pork chop – grilled (broiled), with fat left on	21
– grilled (broiled), with fat removed	9
chicken – roast, meat and skin	12
– roast, meat only	5
– chicken breasts, no skin	3
cheese – Cheddar	20
– Edam	14
– low fat Cheddar	8

fish

Fresh fish is not always easily obtainable. Fishmongers seem to be rare these days, but you may find a local market stall or fish van. The price of fish varies enormously according to the season – it is not such a good buy during the winter months. You can tell if fish really is fresh by its colour and smell. The colour fades as the fish loses its freshness and the eyes look white or sunken. Any unpleasant strong smell should warn you off. Eat fresh fish the day you buy it.

Some of the larger supermarkets have a fresh fish counter, but it is more likely you will have to make do with frozen. As well as the inevitable fish fingers you can buy other packets of breadcrumbed fish. All you need do is grill (broil) them or fry them in a little oil. 'Boil-in-the-bag' fish is just as easy to prepare – as the name suggests, you simply heat the bag in a saucepan of boiling water. In both cases, follow the instructions on the packet.

Frozen fillets of white fish – cod, haddock or plaice (flounder) – should be thawed before cooking. Allow a couple of hours at room temperature, or you can speed things up by holding the fillet under cold running water. Here are the basic ways of cooking a fillet of white fish:

grilling (broiling)

Heat the grill (broiler). Put a knob of butter (or 1 tablespoon oil) into a fireproof dish and put it under the grill to melt. Then remove it and place the fillet in the dish, skin side down. Spoon a little of the melted butter over the fish, and season with salt and pepper. You could also add a little lemon juice or ½ teaspoon of herbs. Put the dish back under the heat for 5–6 minutes, until the fish is cooked (the flesh will flake when you prod it with a fork).

frying

Put 1 tablespoon of flour into a shallow dish and add a pinch of salt and a sprinkling of pepper. Dip the fish in the seasoned flour so that it is completely coated. Heat a little oil or butter in a frying pan (skillet) over a medium heat. Put the fish into the pan and fry on both sides until it is golden. Then reduce the heat and cook for 5–6 minutes.

poaching

Put ¹/₂ cup milk and ¹/₂ cup water into a saucepan and bring it to the boil. Add the fillet of fish, reduce the heat and cover with a lid. Simmer for 5–6 minutes, until the fish flakes when you prod it with a fork.

cod fillet with green pepper

Servings: 1
Time to prepare: 10 minutes

Ingredients	Metric	Imperial	American
cod fillet, fresh or frozen (thaw it first)	*150–225g*	*6–8oz*	*6–8oz*
oil	*1 tbsp*	*1 tbsp*	*1 tbsp*
green (bell) pepper, chopped	*¹/₂*	*¹/₂*	*¹/₂*
tomato sauce	*¹/₂ cup*	*¹/₂ cup*	*¹/₂ cup*
lemon juice	*1 tbsp*	*1 tbsp*	*1 tbsp*
Worcestershire sauce	*1 tsp*	*1 tsp*	*1 tsp*
salt and pepper			

Equipment
Frying pan (skillet) with a lid, fish slice (pancake turner), chopping board, sharp knife

Cooking method
Top of stove

1 Heat the oil in a frying pan (skillet) and fry the green pepper for 3 minutes.
2 Move it to one side of the pan and add the cod fillet.
3 Cook the fish on both sides until lightly browned.
4 Add the tomato sauce, lemon juice and Worcestershire sauce, and season with salt and pepper.
5 Cover with a lid (use a plate if the frying pan does not have one) and cook over a low heat for 5 minutes, or until the fish flakes easily with a fork.

lemon baked fish

Servings: 1
Time to prepare: 30 minutes

Ingredients	Metric	Imperial	American
fillet of cod, haddock, plaice (flounder) or whiting	150–225g	6–8oz	6–8oz
small onion	1	1	1
breadcrumbs	1 tbsp	1 tbsp	1 tbsp
lemon juice	1 tbsp	1 tbsp	1 tbsp
salt and pepper			
a knob of butter			

Equipment
Ovenproof dish, mixing basin, small saucepan, chopping board, knife

Cooking method
Oven

1 Heat the oven to 375°F/190°C Gas Mark 5.
2 Wash the fish in cold water.
3 Peel and chop the onion.

4 Mix together the chopped onion, breadcrumbs, and lemon juice.
5 Season with salt and pepper.
6 Use some of the butter to grease the bottom of an ovenproof dish.
7 Place the fish in the bottom of the dish, skin side down.
8 Spread the breadcrumb mixture on top.
9 Melt the butter in a saucepan over a low heat and pour over the fish.
10 Bake in the oven for 20 minutes.

fish fillet au gratin

Servings: 1
Time to prepare: 45 minutes

Ingredients	Metric	Imperial	American
fillet of cod, haddock, or plaice (flounder)	*150–225g*	*6–8oz*	*6–8oz*
a knob of butter			
tin condensed celery or mushroom soup (undiluted)	*¹/₂*	*¹/₂*	*¹/₂*
grated Cheddar cheese	*1 tbsp*	*1 tbsp*	*1 tbsp*
salt and pepper			
breadcrumbs or crushed cornflakes	*1 tbsp*	*1 tbsp*	*1 tbsp*
grated Parmesan cheese	*2 tsp*	*2 tsp*	*2 tsp*
paprika			

Equipment
Ovenproof dish, small saucepan

Cooking method
Oven

1 Heat the oven to 375°F/190°C Gas Mark 5.
2 Smear a little butter all round an ovenproof dish.
3 Lay the fish fillet in the dish.
4 Put the undiluted soup and Cheddar cheese into a small saucepan, and add salt and pepper to taste.
5 Heat gently until the cheese has melted, then pour over the fish.
6 Mix the breadcrumbs or crushed cornflakes with the Parmesan cheese.
7 Sprinkle on top of the fish, and shake a little paprika over it.
8 Cook in the oven for 30–35 minutes, until the fish flakes readily and the top is bubbly and golden.

kedgeree

Servings: 1
Time to prepare: 15 minutes

Ingredients	Metric	Imperial	American
cooked rice	*1 cup*	*1 cup*	*1 cup*
smoked haddock	*100g*	*4oz*	*4oz*
butter	*1 tbsp*	*1 tbsp*	*1 tbsp*
salt and pepper			
hardboiled egg	*1*	*1*	*1*

Equipment
Saucepan, fish slice (pancake turner)

Cooking method
Top of stove

1 Put the haddock in a saucepan and cover with water.
2 Bring to the boil, reduce the heat, then cover with a lid and simmer for 5–6 minutes until the fish flakes when you prod it with a fork.

3 With a fish slice (pancake turner) lift the haddock out of the saucepan onto a plate.
4 Remove the skin and flake the fish.
5 Rinse out the saucepan and dry it, then put the pan back on the heat and melt the butter in it.
6 Add the cooked rice, flaked fish, salt and pepper and heat through for about 10 minutes.
7 Slice the hard-boiled egg and arrange the slices on top.

herring and mackerel

These come into the category of 'oily' fish, and are supposed to be particularly good for us because the fish oil is thought to reduce cholesterol. They are also the cheapest fish, and the tastiest – if you can cope with the bones. A fishmonger will clean and gut them for you if you buy them fresh, and will remove the centre bones as well if you ask.

herring with mustard sauce

Servings: 1
Time to prepare: 15 minutes

You can also use mackerel for this recipe.

Ingredients	Metric	Imperial	American
herring, gutted and boned	1–2	1–2	1–2
salt and pepper			
medium oatmeal	1 tbsp	1 tbsp	1 tbsp
cooking oil	1 tbsp	1 tbsp	1 tbsp
butter	1 tsp	1 tsp	1 tsp
flour	2 tsp	2 tsp	2 tsp
milk	1 cup	1 cup	1 cup
mustard	1 tsp	1 tsp	1 tsp

Equipment
Frying pan (skillet), small saucepan

Cooking method
Top of stove

1 Wash the fish under cold running water and wipe dry.
2 Season with salt and pepper, and then dip into the oatmeal, pressing it well in on both sides.
3 Heat the oil in a frying pan (skillet) and fry the herring for about 4 minutes on each side, until nicely browned and crisp.
4 Melt the butter in a small saucepan, stir in the flour, and then gradually add the milk. Stir all the time to prevent lumps from forming.
5 When the sauce has thickened stir in the mustard.
6 Serve the fish with the mustard sauce poured over.

food values

There has been a great deal of publicity in recent years about foods that are bad for us. As a result people are changing the way they eat to include more fibre-rich starchy food and less fat, sugar and salt. If you are catering for yourself for the first time it would probably help to have a brief rundown of the nutritive values of food.

proteins

Proteins are necessary for building up new tissue during growth, and for repairing damaged and broken-down cells. They are very complex chemical substances, made up of simpler units called amino acids. There are many different amino acids, but ten of them are essential for growth and repair of body tissues.

If a food contains the ten essential amino acids it is known as 'first class' protein. These are mainly the animal protein foods: meat, fish, eggs, milk and cheese. If a food lacks one or more of the essential amino acids it is known as 'second class protein'. These include nuts, pulses and cereals. If you become a vegetarian and stop eating animal protein, you must replace it with these second class protein foods.

fats

Fats provide fuel and energy for the body, and help to keep you warm. It is not a good idea to cut them out completely, but to change to unsaturated fats. (See the section on Fats and Oils.)

carbohydrates

Carbohydrates are the chief source of energy for the body. Sugar has traditionally been the provider of energy, but we now know that a better supply of energy comes from eating starches – bread (particularly wholemeal), cereals, pasta and potatoes.

vitamins

Vitamins are chemical substances that are found in minute quantities in foodstuffs, and in the past lack of vitamins caused 'deficiency' diseases such as scurvy and rickets. Our diet is so good now that lack of vitamins is almost unknown in this country. Nevertheless it is important not to overcook food, as this will destroy vitamins. Vitamin C in particular is easily lost during the preparation and cooking of food because it is soluble in water and destroyed by heat. Green vegetables and fruit should therefore be eaten raw whenever possible. (See the section on Vitamins.)

minerals

As with vitamins, the lack of any particular mineral element can cause a deficiency disease. The most important minerals in the diet are calcium (found in milk, bread, green vegetables); phosphorus (in meat, fish, dairy products, green vegetables); iron (in fish, vegetables); sulphur (in protein foods, green vegetables, onions); and salt.

Salt (sodium chloride) is necessary for the correct functioning of the muscles and a lack of it can cause cramp. Salt is lost in sweat and in urine and must be replaced. However, salt is used in so many packaged and ready-made foods that we are now getting too much, and it is sensible to cut down the amount we use in cooking or sprinkle onto the food on our plates.

water

Water is continually lost from our bodies by excretion, perspiration and from the lungs, and must be replaced. Anyone who is concerned about the quality of water at home can choose between several varieties of bottled mineral water at the local supermarket.

roughage or fibre

Roughage is composed of cellulose, a complex carbohydrate. It cannot be digested but adds bulk to the diet, helping the elimination and excretion of waste material from the digestive tract. The importance of roughage is now widely recognised. Make sure you get enough by eating wholemeal bread, whole grain cereals, pulses, nuts and fruit and vegetables with their skins still on.

the M *s*

measurements

Most people who read this book will not have kitchen scales, so I have given measurements in spoonfuls and cups – even, in a few cases, handfuls. The only things for which I have given quantities in pounds and ounces (and the metric equivalent) are things you would buy that way, such as meat and vegetables, or sizes of tins. A 'spoonful' in the recipes means a slightly rounded spoonful, unless otherwise stated.

A set of plastic measuring spoons doesn't cost much and is a really useful item to have. It usually includes $1/2$ teaspoon, teaspoon, dessertspoon and tablespoon sizes, also marked in millilitres – 5ml, 10ml and 15ml. You can, of course, use your ordinary spoons.

A measuring jug is useful for liquids, and the best ones also include measures for things like flour and sugar. However, a milk bottle can be used to measure a pint, and most mass-produced mugs hold $1/2$ pint.

Here are some useful measurements:

Flour
1 heaped tablespoon = 25g/1oz

Sugar
1 slightly rounded tablespoon = 25g/1oz

Butter and margarine
1 slightly rounded tablespoon = 25g/1oz
(If the butter is hard, a 2.5cm/1in cube weighs 25g/1oz.)

Cheese
1 heaped tablespoon grated cheese = 15g/½oz
(A 2.5cm/1in cube weighs approximately 25g/1oz.)

Rice
1 slightly rounded tablespoon = 25g/1oz
1 small cup = 100g/4oz

Pasta shapes
1 handful = approx 75g/3oz

Porridge oats
1 heaped tablespoon = 25g/1oz

meat

If you are not used to buying meat, you will find that there is a bewildering choice. What should you buy, how much do you need, and what should you do with it when you've bought it?

It is usual to allow 100-150g (4–6oz) of meat per person; if there is a bone in it then allow 225–350g (8–12oz). Choose the 'cut' of meat that is appropriate to the recipe or cooking method that you are planning to use. Cheap cuts of meat – leg or shin (shank) of beef, hand (shoulder) of pork – are fine for stews and casseroles that you cook for a long time, and they contain just as much protein as more expensive meat. However, it's worth bearing in mind that you use a lot of electricity or gas to cook them, so they may not be much cheaper in the end. For stir-fries and other dishes that require only a short cooking time you must have good quality, tender meat, otherwise you won't be able to get your teeth into it, let alone eat it.

marinating

Meat that is intended for stir-fries or kebabs is vastly improved by marinating, and this will also keep it better in hot weather. A basic marinade is a mixture of wine, vinegar or lemon juice (the acid helps break down the fibres), oil (makes the meat juicier), herbs, salt and pepper (for flavour). Additional ingredients could be soy sauce, tomato purée (paste), chopped onion, carrot or celery. All you have to do is put the marinade ingredients into a bowl, add the meat cut into small pieces, and then stir so that all the meat is coated. Leave it to stand for at least half-an-hour, preferably 3–4 hours, or overnight in the fridge. Drain the meat before you cook it. The marinade can either be used again, or form the basis of a sauce.

storing

Meat goes off very quickly in hot weather, so plan to buy it when you are on your way home, rather than carry it around all day. If you buy the meat in a film-covered tray, store it that way in the refrigerator; otherwise wrap it in foil or greaseproof (wax) paper. Make sure that meat does not come into contact with any other food. Look at the 'best before' or 'sell by' date to see how long you can keep it. Minced (ground) meat should not be kept for longer than a day, but chops and so on will keep a little longer. If you cook meat for eating later it must be cooled as quickly as possible, then covered and refrigerated. Warm food of any kind is an ideal breeding ground for bacteria.

In addition to the recipes below, see also the sections on Casseroles, Stews, and Slow Cooking.

1 ▪ beef

Steak
Not for everyday eating on a limited budget, but you might feel like a special treat occasionally. Steaks are improved if you lay them on a chopping board and beat with a rolling pin or wooden spoon to break down the fibres. The only exception is fillet steak (filet mignon) which is already beautifully tender – and very expensive. Rump, sirloin (rib or loin), and what is called 'frying steak' are cheaper. Minute steak, or flash-fry, has already been beaten to a pulp by the butcher – so don't beat it any more! Minute steak, should be cooked for one minute on each side only.

grilling (broiling)

Heat the grill (broiler). Sprinkle your beaten steak with black pepper and rub with a peeled clove of garlic, if you like it. Put the steak onto the grid of the grill pan and cook on one side. Then turn it over and cook on the other side. If you like your steak rare, 2–3 minutes each side will be enough. For medium or well-done, reduce the heat and cook for a further 3–5 minutes on each side.

frying

Heat a little oil or fat in a frying pan (skillet) over a medium heat. Sprinkle your beaten steak with black pepper and rub with a clove of garlic, if liked. Fry for 1 minute on each side, then turn down the heat and fry gently for another 2–4 minutes each side, according to how well cooked you like it.

minute steak

Servings: 1
Time to prepare: 10 minutes

This is nice with new boiled potatoes and peas or a salad.

Ingredients	Metric	Imperial	American
minute steak	*1*	*1*	*1*
garlic salt and black pepper			
oil	*1 tbsp*	*1 tbsp*	*1 tbsp*
butter	*1 tbsp*	*1 tbsp*	*1 tbsp*
spring onions (scallions), finely chopped	*2*	*2*	*2*
lemon juice	*1 tsp*	*1 tsp*	*1 tsp*
Worcestershire sauce	*1 tsp*	*1 tsp*	*1 tsp*
mustard	*¼ tsp*	*¼ tsp*	*¼ tsp*

Equipment
Frying pan (skillet), chopping board, sharp knife

Cooking method
Top of stove

1 Sprinkle garlic salt and black pepper on both sides of the steak.
2 Heat the oil in a frying pan (skillet) and fry the steak for 2 minutes on each side, on a medium heat.
3 Remove the steak from the frying pan and put it on a warmed plate.

4 Drain the oil from the pan, melt the butter, and add the chopped spring onions (scallions). Fry gently for 2 minutes.

5 Add the lemon juice, Worcestershire sauce and mustard.

6 Heat through gently, then pour the sauce over the steak.

Minced (ground) meat

Minced (ground) meat is a good buy because it is relatively cheap and there are lots of dishes you can make with it. However, even buying minced (ground) meat is complicated these days. A large supermarket will sell fine or coarse ground, depending on whether it has been passed through the mincer (grinder) once or twice, and then you will have to decide on the fat content: usually there will be a choice of 'not more than 10 per cent', '15 per cent' or '20 per cent fat'. Obviously, the less fat there is, the more the meat costs per pound.

Fresh minced (ground) meat should look pink, not brown or grey. You should cook it on the day you buy it, or keep it in the fridge for not more than 24 hours.

As well as the following recipes, see also bolognese sauce; chilli con carne; meat and macaroni; pitta bread filled with mince.

cottage pie

Servings: 1
Time to prepare: 55 minutes

Ingredients	Metric	Imperial	American
minced (ground) beef	100g	4oz	1/2 cup
small onion, peeled and chopped	1	1	1
oil	2 tsp	2 tsp	2 tsp
flour	1 tsp	1 tsp	1 tsp
beef stock (bouillon) cube dissolved in 1/2 cup of hot water	1/2	1/2	1/2
tomato purée (paste)	1 tsp	1 tsp	1 tsp
salt and pepper			
potatoes	2–3	2–3	2–3
a little milk			
a knob of butter or margarine			
grated Cheddar cheese (optional)	1 tbsp	1 tbsp	1 tbsp

Equipment
Frying pan (skillet), saucepan, sieve, ovenproof dish

Cooking method
Top of stove, then grill (broiler)

1 Heat the oil in a frying pan (skillet) and fry the onion gently for 2–3 minutes, until it is soft.
2 Add the meat and continue to fry, stirring all the time, for another 2–3 minutes, or until the meat is brown.
3 Sprinkle the flour over the meat mixture, then stir in the beef stock.
4 Add the tomato purée (paste) and season with salt and pepper.
5 Bring to the boil, then reduce the heat and leave to simmer for 30 minutes.

6 Meanwhile, peel the potatoes, cut them into even-sized pieces and cook in boiling salted water for 15–20 minutes, until they are soft.

7 Drain the potatoes into a sieve, then return them to the saucepan and mash with a fork.

8 Add enough milk to make a smooth mixture.

9 Pour the cooked meat mixture into a fireproof dish.

10 Spoon the mashed potato on top and smooth it down with a fork.

11 Dot the top with little knobs of butter and sprinkle on the cheese if you are using it.

12 Put under a hot grill (broiler) for 2–3 minutes until the top is golden brown.

beefburgers

Servings: 1
Time to prepare: 20 minutes

These taste so much better than commercially-prepared ones. Use a good quality mince with as little fat as possible. Sandwich the burgers between a couple of sesame seed baps, with a slice of cheese if you like it, a lettuce leaf and tomato ketchup or mayonnaise.

Ingredients	Metric	Imperial	American
minced (ground) beef	*100g*	*4oz*	*½ cup*
small onion, finely chopped	*½*	*½*	*½*
rolled oats	*1 tbsp*	*1 tbsp*	*1 tbsp*
dried mixed herbs	*½ tsp*	*½ tsp*	*½ tsp*
salt and pepper			
beaten egg	*1*	*1*	*1*

Equipment
Mixing bowl, fork, chopping board, sharp knife

1 Mix all the ingredients together with a fork, and then gradually add just enough beaten egg to stick everything together – don't make it too wet.
2 Divide the mixture into two portions, and with your hands shape each portion into a ball. Flatten the balls into circles about 1cm/½in thick.
3 Cook the burgers under a hot grill (broiler) for about 5 minutes each side, until they are completely browned and cooked right through.

2 ▪ lamb

Lamb is the meat from a young sheep, up to about a year old; after that it becomes mutton. In the early summer the supermarket shelves display 'New Season Lamb', and this is when English lamb is at its best, and most expensive. At any time of the year, only buy lamb that is dull red, with fat that is hard and white. The best cuts of lamb are leg and shoulder: both are good for roasting, and shoulder makes good kebabs.

shish kebabs

Servings: 1
Time to prepare: 10 minutes

In the summer – barbecue time – you will find that most large supermarkets sell meat already cubed and labelled 'for kebabs'. Often you can buy the kebabs completely made up, but this is a more expensive way of doing it, and less fun. Marinating the meat for a couple of hours before cooking helps to make the meat more tender. All the ingredients should be cut to roughly the same size.

Ingredients

	Metric	Imperial	American
boned lamb	*150g*	*6oz*	*6oz*
French dressing (see page 138)	*2 tbsp*	*2 tbsp*	*2 tbsp*
onion, cut into chunks	*1*	*1*	*1*
tin of pineapple cubes	*200g*	*7oz*	*7oz*
green (bell) pepper, cut into chunks	*¹/₂*	*¹/₂*	*¹/₂*

Equipment
Small bowl, fish slice (pancake turner) or slotted spoon, 2 skewers, chopping board, sharp knife.

Cooking method
Grill (broiler)

1 Cut the meat into 2.5cm/¹/₂in cubes and put into a small basin.
2 Spoon over the French dressing, stir so that all the meat is covered, and leave to marinate for a couple of hours.
3 Remove the meat from the marinade with a fish slice (pancake turner) or slotted spoon and put it onto the skewers, alternating with the onion, pineapple and green pepper.
4 Cook under a hot grill (broiler) for 5 minutes, then turn and cook the other side until the meat is brown and tender.
5 Eat with rice and a salad.

Chops and cutlets
Lamb chops are quick to cook, and make a tasty meal. There are several different types of chop. Loin and chump are the largest, then there are leg chops and cutlets – which are the smallest, and you would probably need two or three. Chops can be grilled (broiled) or fried.

grilling (broiling)

Heat the grill (broiler). Put the chops on the grid of the grill (broiler) pan and cook until the meat has turned brown. Turn the chops over and cook on the other side. The cooking time will depend on how thick the chops are – from 12 to 15 minutes is a rough guide. You can test them by sticking a fork into the meat: it should go in easily and no blood should appear when it is removed.

frying

Heat a little oil or fat in a frying pan (skillet) on medium heat. Put the chops into the pan and fry on one side until brown. Turn over and fry the other side.

mixed grill

Servings: 1
Time to prepare: 30 minutes

Ingredients	Metric	Imperial	American
lamb chop	1	1	1
sausage	1	1	1
rashers streaky bacon (slices)	2	2	2
tomato	1	1	1

Equipment
Grill (broiler) pan

Cooking method
Under the grill (broiler)

1 Put the chop on the grill (broiler) pan and cook under medium heat for 4 minutes.
2 Turn the chop over and cook on the other side for 4 minutes.

3 Put the sausage next to the chop and continue cooking, turning both every few minutes, until the chop is tender and cooked through – test this with a fork.

4 Put the bacon over the chop and sausage.

5 Slice the tomato in half and place next to them.

6 Continue to cook, turning the rashers after 2 minutes.

7 When the bacon and tomato are cooked, remove and serve.

lamb creole

Servings: 1
Time to prepare: 30 minutes

Ingredients	Metric	Imperial	American
lamb chops	*1–2*	*1–2*	*1–2*
flour			
salt and pepper			
a knob of butter			
small onion, finely chopped	*1*	*1*	*1*
tin condensed tomato soup	*1/2*	*1/2*	*1/2*
mixed dried herbs	*1 tsp*	*1 tsp*	*1 tsp*

Equipment
Frying pan (skillet)

Cooking method
Top of stove

1 Put a little flour, seasoned with salt and pepper, onto a plate and coat the chops on both sides with the seasoned flour.

2 Melt the butter in a frying pan (skillet) and fry the onion gently for 3 minutes.

3 Push the onion to one side of the pan and fry the chops on the other side.
4 Pour over the condensed soup, and sprinkle with herbs.
5 Cover with a lid or plate and simmer for 25–30 minutes, until the chops are tender.

3 ▪ pork

Pork is usually cheaper than beef and lamb and should be pale pink, with soft white fat. Pork must be cooked thoroughly and should not be eaten if it is still pink. A chop makes an ideal meal for one person, and can be grilled (broiled) or fried in the same way as a lamb chop, but will need slightly longer cooking time, 15–20 minutes.

pork chop with apple

Servings: 1
Time to prepare: 15–20 minutes

Ingredients	Metric	Imperial	American
pork chop	1	1	1
apple, cut into thick slices	1	1	1
a knob of butter			
sugar	1 tsp	1 tsp	1 tsp

Equipment
Frying pan (skillet), chopping board, sharp knife

Cooking method
Grill (broiler) and top of stove

1 Heat the grill (broiler) to a medium heat.
2 Put the pork chop on the grid of the grill (broiler)

pan and cook for 15–20 minutes, turning to cook both sides.

3 While the chop is cooking, melt the butter in a frying pan (skillet) and fry the apple slices until they are lightly browned.

4 Sprinkle with sugar and continue frying until the edges of the apple are crisp.

5 Serve the fried apple with the grilled chop.

chinese pork

Servings: 1
Time to prepare: 45 minutes

Ingredients	Metric	Imperial	American
pork chop	1	1	1
hoisin sauce	2 tbsp	2 tbsp	2 tbsp
soy sauce	1 tbsp	1 tbsp	1 tbsp
sherry	1 tbsp	1 tbsp	1 tbsp

Equipment
Small basin, ovenproof dish

Cooking method
Oven

1 In a small basin mix together the hoisin sauce, soy sauce and sherry.

2 Put the chop into an ovenproof dish and spread the marinade sauce all over it. Leave to marinate for 2 hours.

3 Cook in a preheated oven (400°F/200°C Gas Mark 6) for 40 minutes.

pork and beans

Servings: 1
Time to prepare: 1 hour

Ingredients	Metric	Imperial	American
lean pork, cubed	100–150g	4–6oz	4–6oz
oil	2 tsp	2 tsp	2 tsp
small onion, peeled and finely chopped	1	1	1
chicken stock (bouillon) cube dissolved in 2 tablespoons hot water	$\frac{1}{2}$	$\frac{1}{2}$	$\frac{1}{2}$
tomato purée (paste)	1 tsp	1 tsp	1 tsp
small tin baked beans	1	1	1

Equipment
Saucepan, chopping board, knife

Cooking method
Top of stove

1 Heat the oil in a saucepan and quickly fry the pork for a couple of minutes, stirring all the time.
2 Add the onion and cook for another minute.
3 Add the stock and tomato purée (paste).
4 Bring to the boil, then lower the heat, cover with a lid and simmer for 45 minutes.
5 Stir in the baked beans and heat through for another 5 minutes.

microwave

Microwave cooking needs a whole book to itself, but in case you have access to a microwave oven and are not sure how to use it, a few notes might be helpful.

A microwave oven on its own cannot replace the conventional cooker – it is used to best advantage in conjunction with other cooking methods. However, it is particularly good for cooking small quantities, so is useful for someone living on their own.

Its advantages are speed – a jacket potato cooks in only 4 minutes instead of an hour in a conventional oven; economy – the energy is directed straight into the food and not wasted on heating the cooking container or the oven walls; versatility – one piece of equipment can defrost, reheat, boil, bake, roast and poach; and it is labour saving – food can be cooked in the serving dish, which cuts down on washing-up.

On the minus side, browning and crisping are difficult in a microwave, so that food often comes out looking insipid. And microwaves are no good for tougher cuts of meat, which need cooking slowly.

A microwave is useful for reheating cold meals and cups of coffee; defrosting food quickly; cooking ready-prepared meals; and the suggestions below. NEVER use metal containers – china, glass and most other non-metal containers are suitable. Microwave cling-film (plastic wrap) can be used to cover food so that it doesn't dry out. Always leave food to stand for a few minutes after it has finished cooking – this is an essential part of the process.

fish

A microwave oven is wonderful for cooking fish. All you have to do is put the fish – either a whole round one such as trout, or a flat fillet of plaice or other white fish – between two plates and cook on High for 3 minutes. Thicker cutlets and steaks need a little longer.

scrambled eggs

Break an egg into a small basin, add a little milk and beat with a fork. Cook on High for 1 minute, remove from the oven and stir, then cook for another 30 seconds. Add salt and pepper after cooking, not before.

porridge

Put 1 cupful of porridge oats and 2–2½ cups of water into a bowl, stir, and cook on High for 2 minutes. Remove from the oven and stir well, then cook for another minute.

jacket potato

Scrub the potato, dry it, and prick in several places with a fork. Cook on High for 4 minutes. Test with a fork to see if it is soft, and if not cook for a further minute.

the **P** s

pancakes

Pancakes are traditionally eaten on Shrove Tuesday (Pancake Day), usually sprinkled with sugar and lemon juice, or perhaps with golden (corn) syrup dribbled over the top. Another way of eating pancakes is to stuff them with a savoury filling to make a complete meal.

The basic recipe for batter given below is enough for 6–8 pancakes. Once you have made the pancakes, they can be stored for a week in the fridge (or they can be frozen), so it is a good idea to make more than you need for one meal. You might, for example, have sweet pancakes for pudding one day, and do savoury pancakes for a main meal the next.

If you have time, it is better to let the batter stand for an hour before using it. This allows the flour to absorb the liquid and the pancakes will be light. However, this is not essential.

basic recipe for batter

Makes: 6–8 pancakes

Ingredients	Metric	Imperial	American
plain (all-purpose) flour	4 tbsp	4 tbsp	4 tbsp
a pinch of salt			
egg	1	1	1
milk	300ml	1/2pt	1 1/4 cups

Equipment
Mixing bowl, wooden spoon, frying pan (skillet), fish slice (pancake turner)

Cooking method
Top of stove

1 Put the flour and salt into a mixing bowl.
2 Make a well in the centre of the flour and break the egg into it.
3 Using a wooden spoon, stir the egg and draw in the flour from around the side.
4 Gradually add just enough milk to incorporate all the flour and make a thick paste.
5 Beat very well to remove all the lumps so that the mixture is smooth.
6 Stir in the remaining milk, a little at a time.
7 Beat the batter thoroughly until small air bubbles appear all over the surface.
8 Leave the batter to stand for up to an hour, if you have time.

To make pancakes
1 Heat a frying pan (skillet) until it is really hot.
2 Put in 1/2 teaspoon of oil or a small knob of butter and allow this to spread all around the pan.
3 Pour in a little batter and tilt the pan so that it runs all over the base – it should make a very thin layer.

103

4 Let the pancake cook for about 1 minute, shaking the pan a little to stop it sticking, until the top is just set and the underneath is lightly browned.

5 Use a fish slice (pancake turner) or spatula to turn the pancake over (or toss it, if you dare!).

6 Cook for about another 20 seconds until the other side is browned, then turn the pancake out onto a plate.

7 If you are making several pancakes to use later, stack them with greaseproof (wax) paper in between, so that they do not stick together.

sweet pancakes

To reheat pancakes that you have stored in the fridge, put them between two plates on top of a pan of simmering water; or warm them under the grill (broiler). Add your filling and then roll the pancake up or fold it over.

Suggested fillings

Sugar and lemon juice

Golden (corn) syrup, honey or jam

Fresh fruit – sliced banana, strawberries, etc

Chocolate spread, or sprinkle over a tablespoon of drinking chocolate

savoury pancakes

For a main meal allow yourself 2 or 3 pancakes. Put a tablespoon of filling in the centre of each one and roll it up. Arrange the pancakes in a shallow dish and sprinkle a tablespoon of grated Cheddar cheese on top, then dot with a few knobs of butter or margarine. Put the dish under the grill (broiler) set on moderate heat, or heat in the oven for 10 minutes at 400°F/ 200°C Gas Mark 6.

Suggested fillings

Cooked chicken and sweetcorn, with a little tomato ketchup

Bacon and mushrooms, fried first in a little oil or butter

Minced (ground) beef, fried with a little onion and mixed with a spoonful of tomato purée (paste)

Asparagus tips (tinned), heated through and drained

pasta

Pasta is a nutritious and healthy food – ideal for people on a low budget or with limited cooking facilities. It is cheap, quick and easy to cook, keeps well in the store cupboard, and is endlessly versatile.

1 ▪ pasta for boiling

Spaghetti: Long, thin, string-like pasta. Comes in various lengths and thicknesses.

Tagliatelli: Flat, ribbon noodles, made from egg pasta. Comes in strands or nests. There is also a green version, coloured with spinach juice.

Macaroni: Slightly curved tube pasta of varying sizes and lengths.

Rigatoni: Fat tube pasta with ridges.

Shapes: Shells (*conchiglie*), bows (*farfelle*), twists (*fusilli*), and tubes (*penne*) come in various sizes, smooth or ridged.

These will all have cooking instructions on the packet. The method is the same for fresh or dried pasta, but the time required will be different – fresh pasta takes about 3 minutes, dried about 12 minutes.

If you have a normal appetite allow 100g/4oz dried pasta for a main course – more if you are a big eater. If you don't have scales, a handful of pasta shapes weighs about 50g/2oz. Or (for spaghetti and tagliatelli) you can work out how much you need to use by noting the weight in the packet and calculating accordingly.

Bring to the boil a large saucepan of boiling water (you can speed this up by boiling water in a kettle and then pouring it into the saucepan). Add salt and a few drops of cooking oil, which will help stop the water boiling over. Then put in the pasta – long spaghetti or tagliatelli should be stood up in the saucepan and then pushed down gradually as it softens. Let the water come to the boil again, then lower the heat a little and leave to simmer (without a lid) until the pasta is just cooked. The pasta should have a slight bite to it, which the Italians call *al dente*. Drain the pasta in a sieve and eat it in one of the following ways:

Plain
Pasta tastes delicious just on its own. Put a knob of butter or a little olive oil on top of the hot cooked pasta, and then sprinkle on some black pepper – preferably freshly ground.

Parmesan cheese
Sprinkle over the hot cooked pasta. A drum of Parmesan cheese keeps for a long time in the fridge and goes a long way.

Pesto
Pesto is a strong, tangy sauce made from basil and pine nuts. Stir about a tablespoonful into your hot cooked pasta, and if you like it sprinkle some Parmesan cheese on top. You can buy pesto in a small jar, which should be kept in the fridge once it is opened.

Ready-made tomato and Bolognese sauces
Careful inspection of the supermarket shelves will reveal a variety of tins and jars containing ready-made sauces to pour over your pasta. Keep a few of these in your store cupboard along with the dried pasta and you will always have an instant, satisfying meal available. Experiment with the various brands – some are much better than others.

make your own Bolognese sauce

Servings: 1
Time to prepare: 40 minutes

This is the simplest way of making your own Bolognese sauce if you don't want to use a ready-made one. You can also use this sauce to make lasagna (see below).

Ingredients	Metric	Imperial	American
pasta	*100g*	*4oz*	*1 cup*
oil	*2 tsp*	*2 tsp*	*2 tsp*
small onion	*1*	*1*	*1*
minced (ground) beef	*100g*	*4oz*	*½ cup*
tomatoes	*2*	*2*	*2*
tomato purée (paste)	*1 tbsp*	*1 tbsp*	*1 tbsp*
water	*1 tbsp*	*1 tbsp*	*1 tbsp*
salt and pepper			
dried herbs (optional)	*1 tsp*	*1 tsp*	*1 tsp*

Equipment
2 saucepans, sieve, chopping board, sharp knife

Cooking method
Top of stove

1 Heat the oil in a saucepan.
2 Peel and slice the onion and fry gently for 2–3 minutes.
3 Turn up the heat a little and add the beef.
4 Fry the meat until it is light brown in colour, stirring all the time.
5 Chop the tomatoes and add to the meat mixture along with the tomato purée (paste) and water.
6 Season with salt and pepper, and add the dried herbs if you are using them.
7 Turn down the heat so that the sauce simmers.
8 Put on the lid and leave to cook for 30 minutes.
9 Meanwhile cook the pasta in another saucepan.
10 Drain the pasta and spoon the cooked sauce on top.
11 Sprinkle on some Parmesan cheese.

tuna pasta

Servings: 1
Time to prepare: 20 minutes

This recipe uses things from your store cupboard, so it's useful for when you don't have time to go shopping for fresh ingredients.

Ingredients	Metric	Imperial	American
pasta	100g	4oz	1 cup
small tin tuna in brine	1	1	1
small tin chopped tomatoes	1	1	1
a pinch of mixed dried herbs			
black pepper			

Equipment
Saucepan, sieve

Cooking method
Top of stove

1 Cook the pasta first, and drain it in the sieve.
2 Rinse out the saucepan and dry it.
3 Drain the tuna and put it into the saucepan with the tomatoes and herbs.
4 Heat gently for 5 minutes.
5 Add the drained, cooked pasta and mix everything together thoroughly.
6 Sprinkle with black pepper.

macaroni cheese

Servings: 1
Time to prepare: 30 minutes

This is usually made with *maccheroni*, but you can use any of the pasta shapes instead. The easiest way to make this dish it to use a packet of cheese sauce mix – make it up according to the instructions and stir in some cooked pasta. However, it's no bad thing to learn how to make cheese sauce yourself, and the instructions are given below.

Ingredients	Metric	Imperial	American
(a good handful) macaroni or pasta shapes, cooked	*75g*	*3oz*	*³/₄ cup*
butter	*1 tsp*	*1 tsp*	*1 tsp*
flour	*2 tsp*	*2 tsp*	*2 tsp*
milk	*1 cup*	*1 cup*	*1 cup*
salt and pepper			
mustard	*¹/₂ tsp*	*¹/₂ tsp*	*¹/₂ tsp*
grated Cheddar cheese	*3 tbsp*	*3 tbsp*	*3 tbsp*

Equipment
Saucepan, sieve, cheese grater, fireproof (e.g. Pyrex) dish

Cooking method
Top of stove, then grill (broiler)

1 Cook the macaroni or pasta shapes and drain into a sieve.
2 Rinse out the saucepan and dry it.
3 Put the butter into the saucepan and heat gently until it has just melted – do not allow it to go brown.
4 Stir in the flour and cook gently for 1 minute.
5 Remove the pan from the heat and very gradually stir in the milk. (This is the tricky bit – if you don't stir thoroughly you will get horrible lumps instead of a smooth sauce!)
6 Return the pan to the heat and, still stirring, bring the sauce to the boil.
7 The sauce will now have thickened. Remove it from the heat and stir in half the grated cheese, the cooked pasta, and the mustard.
8 Season with salt and pepper.
9 Spoon the macaroni cheese into a fireproof dish and sprinkle the remaining cheese on top.
10 Put under a hot grill (broiler) for a few minutes until the top is browned and bubbling.

● *You can add other ingredients to this dish. For variety try adding some chopped ham or cooked bacon, sliced cooked mushrooms, or some slices of tomato on top.*

pasta carbonara

Servings: 1
Time to prepare: 20 minutes

This is an adaptation of the traditional Roman dish. It's really easy to make, simply delicious, and uses up odds and ends from the fridge.

Ingredients	Metric	Imperial	American
pasta	*100g*	*4oz*	*1 cup*
oil	*1 tbsp*	*1 tbsp*	*1 tbsp*
slice of ham, or a couple of rashers (slices) of bacon	*1*	*1*	*1*
beaten egg	*1*	*1*	*1*
grated Cheddar cheese	*1 tbsp*	*1 tbsp*	*1 tbsp*
black pepper			

Equipment
Saucepan, sieve, small basin, cheese grater

Cooking method
Top of stove

1 Cook the pasta first, then drain it into the sieve.
2 Rinse out and dry the saucepan, then heat the oil.
3 Chop the ham or bacon into small pieces and fry gently for 3–4 minutes.
4 Add the cooked pasta and stir well, then add the beaten egg and the grated cheese.
5 Stir everything thoroughly so that it all gets mixed together.
6 The egg will cook while you are doing this, and the cheese will melt, so that all the ingredients will stick together.
7 Turn the pasta out onto a warm plate and sprinkle with plenty of black pepper.

2 ▪ stuffed pasta

Ravioli: Pasta squares with serrated edges, traditionally filled with spinach and ricotta cheese, but often nowadays with meat. You can buy fresh stuffed ravioli, or there is a tinned variety in tomato sauce.

Cannelloni: Large, short tubes for stuffing and then baking, usually bought in the dried form. In some supermarkets you can buy it fresh, ready-stuffed, for baking yourself.

3 ▪ baked pasta

Lasagna: Broad sheets of egg pasta for baking, which can be bought pre-cooked or fresh. Lasagna sometimes has wavy edges, and there is a green version.

lasagna

Servings: 1
Time to prepare: 35 minutes

This dish consists of some sheets of lasagna layered alternately with Bolognese sauce and cheese sauce. Use a tin or jar of Bolognese sauce, or the recipe given earlier; and for the cheese sauce use a packet mix or follow the instructions given for macaroni cheese.

Ingredients	Metric	Imperial	American
sheets of lasagna	4	4	4
tin or jar of Bolognese sauce	1	1	1
cheese sauce mix			
grated Cheddar cheese	1 tbsp	1 tbsp	1 tbsp

Equipment
Ovenproof dish

Cooking method
Oven

1 Preheat the oven to 400°F/200°C Gas Mark 6.
2 Make up the cheese sauce according to the instructions on the packet and pour one third of it into an ovenproof dish.
3 Arrange two sheets of lasagna on top.
4 Add half the Bolognese sauce.
5 Repeat these layers, finishing with a final layer of cheese sauce.
6 Top with grated cheese.
7 Bake in the oven for about 30 minutes, until the cheese on top is golden brown and bubbling.

4 ▪ pasta for soups

There are all kinds of pasta shapes to add to soups – letters, shells, rings, stars and so on. Clear soups are best with tiny pasta shapes, whereas a hearty soup like minestrone will take something bigger and thicker.

Italian bean and pasta soup

Servings: 2
Time to prepare: 25 minutes

This makes enough for two servings – you can reheat the second portion.

Ingredients	Metric	Imperial	American
oil	1 tbsp	1 tbsp	1 tbsp
small onion, finely chopped	1	1	1
clove of garlic, crushed	1	1	1
carrot, finely diced	1	1	1
stick of celery, finely sliced	1	1	1
tomato purée (paste)	2 tsp	2 tsp	2 tsp
beef stock, made with a stock (bouillon) cube put into boiling water	600ml	1pt	2$^{1}/_{2}$ cups
tin borlotti beans	200g	7oz	7oz
small pasta shapes (a handful)	50g	2oz	$^{1}/_{2}$ cup
frozen or tinned peas	$^{1}/_{2}$ cup	$^{1}/_{2}$ cup	$^{1}/_{2}$ cup
salt and pepper			

Equipment
Saucepan, chopping board, sharp knife

Cooking method
Top of stove

1 Heat the oil in a saucepan.
2 Add the onion, garlic, carrot and celery and cook gently for 5 minutes.
3 Add the tomato purée (paste), stock and beans.
4 Bring to the boil and simmer for 10 minutes.
5 Add the pasta and peas and cook for a further 7 minutes, until the pasta is just cooked.
6 Add salt and pepper to taste.
7 Serve hot.

pizzas

Why make your own when you can buy a take-away? Making your own is cheaper, you can have exactly the topping you want – and, above all, it's fun. There are two ways of making pizzas: the easy way, using self-raising flour; and the more difficult, but 'proper' way, using yeast. The amounts given will satisfy one really hungry person, or two with normal appetites.

easy pizza

Servings: 1–2
Time to prepare: 30 minutes

Ingredients	Metric	Imperial	American
self-raising flour	4 tbsp	4 tbsp	1 cup
salt	½ tsp	½ tsp	½ tsp
margarine	1 tbsp	1 tbsp	1 tbsp
milk	2–3 tbsp	2–3 tbsp	2–3 tbsp

Equipment
Mixing basin, rolling pin (or milk bottle), baking tray

Cooking method
Oven

1 Heat the oven to 400°F/200°C Gas Mark 6.
2 Grease a baking tray.
3 Put the flour, salt and margarine into a mixing basin.
4 Rub the margarine into the flour with your fingertips, until the mixture looks like breadcrumbs.
5 Add enough milk to make the mixture into a firm ball of dough.

6 Sprinkle some flour onto a suitable surface and on this roll out the ball of dough into a circle about 15cm/6in in diameter.
7 Put the pizza base onto the greased baking tray.
8 Add the topping of your choice.
9 Bake in the preheated oven for about 20 minutes, until the edges of the pizza are golden brown.

proper pizza

Servings: 1–2
Time to prepare: 1¼ hours

Ingredients	Metric	Imperial	American
dried yeast (active)	1 tsp	1 tsp	1 tsp
sugar	½ tsp	½ tsp	½ tsp
warm water	5 tbsp	5 tbsp	5 tbsp
plain (all-purpose) flour	4 tbsp	4 tbsp	4 tbsp
salt	½ tsp	½ tsp	½ tsp

Equipment
Measuring jug, mixing basin, rolling pin (or milk bottle), baking tray

Cooking method
Oven

1 Heat the oven to 425°F/220°C Gas Mark 7.
2 Grease a baking tray.
3 Put the warm water into a jug and stir in the dried yeast and sugar.
4 Leave in a warm place for 10–15 minutes, until the yeast has dissolved and the liquid is frothy.
5 Put the flour and salt into a mixing basin.
6 Make a well in the centre and pour in the frothing liquid.

7 Mix until you have a soft dough.
8 Sprinkle some flour onto a suitable surface and knead the dough for 5 minutes.
9 Sprinkle some flour around the mixing basin, put the dough back in and cover the basin with a damp teacloth.
10 Leave it in a warm place for about 30 minutes, until the dough has doubled in size.
11 Knead the dough again for a couple of minutes on the floured surface.
12 Roll out to a circle 15cm/6in in diameter.
13 Put the pizza base onto the greased baking tray.
14 Add the topping of your choice.
15 Bake in the oven for 20 minutes, or until the edges of the pizza are golden brown.

suggested toppings

The best cheese to use is mozzarella, but Cheddar will do. Parmesan cheese sprinkled on top gives a stronger cheese flavour. Invent your own toppings from any of the ingredients below, or try new ones.

Mushroom, tomato and cheese: Peel and slice mushrooms, slice tomatoes, grate cheese on top.
Tomato, salami and cheese: Slice tomatoes and sprinkle with salt and pepper. Arrange slices of salami and cheese on top.
Onion, sweetcorn and cheese: Peel and slice the onion into very thin rings. Spoon some drained sweetcorn over the onions. Grate cheese on top.
Tuna, onion and cheese: Peel and slice the onion and fry until soft. Spread over pizza base and add the tuna. Grate cheese on top.

garnishes

Anchovies, sardines, olives, thin strips of green (bell) pepper, fresh or dried herbs.

pizza base mix

In most supermarkets you can buy packets of pizza base mix. You simply add water to the mix, knead, roll out and top with your choice of ingredients. It's a good idea to keep a packet in your store cupboard. Here is a quick recipe that uses a prepared pizza base mix. Mozzarella cheese and Parma ham are usually available in large supermarkets or delicatessens. If you can't find them, you can use Cheddar or Gruyère cheese, and ordinary ham.

Ingredients	Metric	Imperial	American
packet pizza base mix	1	1	1
oil (sunflower or olive)	1 tbsp	1 tbsp	1 tbsp
mozzarella (Cheddar or Gruyère) cheese, thinly sliced			
Parma (or ordinary) ham, sliced			
salt and pepper			

Equipment
Large frying pan (skillet), fish slice (pancake turner)

Cooking method
Top of stove and grill (broiler)

1 Make up the pizza base mix according to the instructions on the packet.
2 Roll out to the size of your frying pan (skillet).
3 Heat the oil in the frying pan and then add the pizza base.
4 Cook on a medium heat for 5–10 minutes, until the base of the pizza is crisp, firm and golden brown.
5 Use a fish slice (pancake turner) to turn the pizza over.
6 Lay slices of cheese and ham on top.
7 Season with plenty of salt and pepper.

8 Cook for a further 5–10 minutes until the underside of the pizza is crisp and firm.
9 Put the pizza under a preheated hot grill (broiler) and cook for a few minutes until the cheese has completely melted and started to bubble and turn golden brown.

potatoes

Contrary to popular belief, plain boiled or baked potatoes are low in calories and are, in fact, a very nutritious food – they contain protein as well as carbohydrates, vitamin C, essential minerals and dietary fibre. There are quite a few different varieties of potato, and the supermarket will probably have a choice of 'red' or 'white', referring to the colour of the skin. Generally speaking, the white ones are better for baking and the red for boiling. Potatoes will keep well for several weeks if you take them out of the plastic bag they were sold in and transfer them to a brown paper bag or cardboard box. Store them in a cool, dry, airy place. 'New' potatoes are best used soon after buying them.

boiled potatoes

If you are using small new potatoes, scrub them thoroughly and leave them whole with the skins on. Old potatoes should be peeled and cut into even-sized pieces. Put the potatoes into a saucepan and cover with hot water. Add a pinch of salt. Put the pan onto a high heat and bring to the boil. Then reduce the heat, cover with a lid and simmer for 10–20 minutes until the potatoes are soft (you can test them with a fork). New potatoes cook much more quickly than old ones. Drain the potatoes into a sieve.

mashed potatoes

Boil some old potatoes as described on previous page. Drain through a sieve and return them to the pan. Add a little milk and a knob of butter. Mash with a fork until the potato is smooth.

sauté potatoes

Boil some potatoes as described above, but slightly reduce the cooking time so that they are still firm and have not broken up. Cut them into 5mm/$\frac{1}{4}$in slices. Heat 2 tablespoons oil in a frying pan (skillet), and when it is hot add the slices of potato. Fry quickly for about 2 minutes, then turn them over and cook the other side. Sprinkle with salt and pepper before serving.

chips (French fries)

If you must have chips it is much easier, safer and healthier to buy the oven-ready ones. These can be cooked in the oven or under the grill (broiler) – follow the instructions on the packet.

scalloped potatoes

These go really well with a chicken casserole (see page 44), and you will be making good use of the oven by cooking two dishes at once. Smear some butter round an ovenproof dish. Peel and slice 2 large potatoes and chop a small onion. Arrange the potato slices in the dish, and cover with the onion. Add $\frac{1}{2}$ cup of milk. Put a knob of butter on top, and sprinkle on 1 tablespoon of grated Cheddar cheese. Cover with a lid or foil and cook in the oven (375°F/190°C Gas Mark 5) for about an hour. Remove the lid 15 minutes before the end of cooking time to brown the top.

jacket potatoes

You need a large, well-shaped potato – supermarkets now sell potatoes specifically for baking. Scrub the potato well and dry it. Prick it all over with a fork and smear a little oil or butter over the skin. Bake in a hot oven (400°F/200°C Gas Mark 6) for 1–1¹/₂ hours, until the centre is soft and fluffy. If you spear it with a skewer it will cook more quickly.

A jacket potato goes well with any kind of meal. If you already have the oven on to cook a casserole you might as well do a potato at the same time. To serve, cut the potato in half, put a knob of butter or margarine on each half and sprinkle with salt and pepper. Here are some fillings for jacket potatoes:

Baked beans: Heat the beans and spoon over the potato.
Bolognese sauce (see page 107): Spoon the hot sauce over the potato.
Cheese: Sprinkle a tablespoon of grated Cheddar cheese over each half. You could then brown it under the grill (broiler).
Chilli con carne (see page 26): Spoon over the potato.
Cottage cheese: A tablespoon of cottage cheese, piled on top of each half, for those who are watching calories.
Bacon: Cut 1 or 2 rashers (slices) of bacon into small pieces and fry until crisp. Remove potato flesh from the skin, mix in the chopped bacon, return the mixture to the skin, and put under the grill (broiler) for a few minutes to brown.
Egg: Remove potato flesh from the skin, mash with a little butter. Put a little potato back in one half and break an egg onto the potato. Heap more potato on top to fill the case. Put rest of potato in other case. Return to oven for 15 minutes to cook the egg.

Scrambled egg: Scoop a hollow in each side of the potato and spoon in scrambled egg.

Sardines: Remove potato flesh from skin. Mix in two sardines. Return mixture to the skins. Return to oven for 5 minutes.

● *If you have access to a microwave oven you can cook a potato in only 5–7 minutes, on the high setting (see Microwave Oven).*

Here are some ideas for using up cooked potatoes.

potato cakes

Servings: 1
Time to prepare: 10 minutes

Ingredients	Metric	Imperial	American
cooked, mashed potato	4 tbsp	4 tbsp	4 tbsp
flour	2 tsp	2 tsp	2 tsp
salt and pepper			
cooking oil	1 tbsp	1 tbsp	1 tbsp

Equipment
Frying pan (skillet), mixing bowl, chopping board, fish slice (pancake turner)

Cooking method
Top of stove

1 Mix the flour into the mashed potato and season well with salt and pepper.
2 Sprinkle some flour onto a chopping board.
3 Divide the potato mixture into two or three pieces and on the floured board form each piece into a flattened cake, about 1cm/¹/₂in thick.

4 Heat the oil in a frying pan (skillet).
5 Fry the potato cakes until they are golden brown, 3–4 minutes on each side.

bubble and squeak

Servings: 1
Time to prepare: 10 minutes

Ingredients	Metric	Imperial	American
cooked, mashed potato	*4 tbsp*	*4 tbsp*	*4 tbsp*
cold, cooked green vegetables (cabbage, sprouts, etc)			
salt and pepper			
cooking oil	*1 tbsp*	*1 tbsp*	*1 tbsp*

Equipment
Frying pan (skillet), mixing bowl, chopping board, knife, fish slice (pancake turner)

Cooking method
Top of stove

1 Chop up the cooked green vegetables and mix with the mashed potato.
2 Season well with salt and pepper.
3 Heat the oil in a frying pan (skillet).
4 Fry bubble and squeak until golden brown underneath.
5 Turn over and fry the other side.
6 Serve with fried bacon or sausages.

corned beef hash

Servings: 1
Time to prepare: 20 minutes

Ingredients	Metric	Imperial	American
mashed potato	*4 tbsp*	*4 tbsp*	*4 tbsp*
egg	*1*	*1*	*1*
slices corned beef (cooked)	*2*	*2*	*2*
small onion	*1*	*1*	*1*
salt and pepper			
cooking oil	*1 tbsp*	*1 tbsp*	*1 tbsp*

Equipment
Frying pan (skillet), mixing basin, chopping board, knife, fish slice (pancake turner)

Cooking method
Top of stove

1 Beat the egg and add to the mashed potato.
2 Season with salt and pepper.
3 Dice the corned beef.
4 Peel and finely chop the onion.
5 Heat the oil in the frying pan (skillet) and fry the onion until soft.
6 Add potato and corned beef, spreading it over the bottom of the pan.
7 Cook until the underside is brown and the mixture is really hot.

puddings

There is really no need to worry about cooking puddings. The shops are full of chilled and frozen desserts, packet mixes, ready-made pies and tarts – or you can eat fruit. Here are a few simple desserts if you feel like making something yourself.

old-fashioned chocolate pudding

Servings: 2
Time to prepare: 10 minutes

This is better than any of the chocolate whips you buy in a packet, and just as easy to make. The second helping will keep in the fridge for the following day.

Ingredients	Metric	Imperial	American
cornflour (corn starch)	*1 tbsp*	*1 tbsp*	*1 tbsp*
cocoa powder (unsweetened)	*1 tbsp*	*1 tbsp*	*1 tbsp*
sugar	*1 tbsp*	*1 tbsp*	*1 tbsp*
milk	*300 ml*	*¹/₂ pt*	*1¹/₄ cups*

Equipment
Small basin, small saucepan

Cooking method
Top of stove

1 Put the cornflour (corn starch), cocoa powder and sugar into a small basin and stir in enough milk to make a thinnish paste. Make sure the ingredients are really well mixed, particularly the cornflour.
2 Pour the remaining milk into a small saucepan and heat until almost boiling.

3 Stir the hot milk into the chocolate mixture.
4 Mix well and pour the whole lot back into the saucepan.
5 Put on a moderate heat and stir continuously until the mixture is boiling and has thickened.
6 Remove from the heat and pour into the basin.
7 Sprinkle a little sugar on top to prevent a skin forming.
8 Eat warm or cold, with a little milk or cream.

baked apple

Servings: 1
Time to prepare: 45 minutes

This is only worth doing if you have the oven on anyway.

Ingredients	Metric	Imperial	American
large cooking (tart) apple	1	1	1
dried fruit	1 tbsp	1 tbsp	1 tbsp
brown sugar	1 tsp	1 tsp	1 tsp
a knob of butter			

Equipment
Small ovenproof dish, sharp knife

Cooking method
Oven

1 Wash the apple, cut out the core and score a line round the centre with a knife.
2 Stand the apple in a small ovenproof dish.
3 Stuff the centre with dried fruit and brown sugar, and put a knob of butter on top.
4 Pour a tablespoon of water around the apple.
5 Bake in the oven for 30–40 minutes until the apple is soft.

banana custard

Servings: 1–2
Time to prepare: 10 minutes

If you don't eat all this at one sitting, the second portion will keep all right in the fridge until the following day. You can use a tin of ready-made custard instead of making your own.

Ingredients	Metric	Imperial	American
banana	*1*	*1*	*1*
custard powder (Bird's English dessert mix)	*1 tbsp*	*1 tbsp*	*1 tbsp*
sugar	*¹/₂ tbsp*	*¹/₂ tbsp*	*¹/₂ tbsp*
milk	*300 ml*	*¹/₂ pt*	*1¹/₂ cups*

Equipment
Small basin, small saucepan

Cooking method
Top of stove

1 Put the custard powder (dessert mix) and sugar into a small basin and stir in enough milk to make a thinnish paste.
2 Pour the remaining milk into a small saucepan and heat until it is just boiling.
3 Pour the boiling milk onto the custard mixture, stirring briskly until the custard thickens.
4 Peel and chop the banana and stir into the custard.

fruit fritters

Servings: 1
Time to prepare: 15 minutes

For fritters, make batter in the same way as for pancakes (see page 102), but use half the amount of milk, so that the batter is thicker.

Ingredients	Metric	Imperial	American
thick batter			
cooking (tart) apple, or	*1*	*1*	*1*
1 banana, or 2 pineapple rings			
from a tin			
oil for frying			

Equipment
Mixing basin, sharp knife, frying pan (skillet), fish slice (pancake turner) or slotted spoon

Cooking method
Top of stove

1 Peel the apple, remove the core and slice into 5mm/¹/₄in thick rings. (Or slice the banana in half lengthways, then in half across to make four pieces; drain the pineapple rings from the tin.)
2 Put about 1cm/¹/₂in oil in a frying pan (skillet) and heat until a faint smoke is rising from it.
3 Dip the pieces of fruit in the batter so that they are thickly coated, and then lower them into the hot oil.
4 Fry the fritters until they are a deep golden brown, then lift out with a fish slice (pancake turner) and drain on kitchen paper.
5 Sprinkle with sugar while still hot.

the **R** *s*

refrigerator

Milk, butter, cheese, eggs, meat, fish and other perishable foods should be kept in a refrigerator. The low temperature reduces the activity of micro-organisms and enzymes which cause deterioration. It also dries out food, so everything needs to be wrapped in cling film (plastic wrap) or foil, or kept in a plastic container. Milk should always be covered as it picks up the smell and flavour of other foods. Salad vegetables can be kept in the vegetable box or a plastic bag.

If you have a refrigerator with a frozen food compartment at the top you can store packets of frozen vegetables, ice cream, beefburgers, and so on. It's also handy to be able to freeze part of a loaf for future consumption – or to make double the amount of Bolognese sauce, for example, and freeze half for a later meal.

The length of time frozen food can safely be kept varies: 3-star fridges keep frozen food for up to 3 months; 2-star fridges up to 1 month; 1-star fridges up to 1 week. Frozen food will keep for a day or two in the refrigerator. Once thawed, the food should never be refrozen.

defrosting

Refrigerators have to be defrosted regularly, unless you are lucky enough to have one that does this automatically, otherwise deposits of frost form round the freezing unit, and this reduces efficiency. Eventually, one day, you won't be able to get the door shut. Ideally defrosting should be done once a week, but realistically you are not likely to do it more than once a month. Here's what you do:

1 Switch off the fridge, or turn the thermostat to the index mark specified in the maker's instructions.
2 Remove all the food. Frozen food can be wrapped in several layers of newspaper to stop it defrosting.
3 Place a drip tray under the freezing unit.
4 Remove ice trays, empty and refill with fresh water.
5 Remove shelves, wash in warm water and dry well.
6 Place a bowl of hot water inside the fridge to speed up defrosting. Deposits of ice can be removed with a plastic scraper – never use a metal knife or you might stab a hole in the cabinet.
7 When all the frost has melted, wipe the inside of the cabinet with a clean cloth. If it needs a thorough cleaning, use a weak solution of sodium bicarbonate or of borax – about 1 tablespoon of bicarbonate or 1 teaspoon of borax to 1 gallon (10 pints) of water. Do not use soap or washing-up liquid.
8 Dry thoroughly and replace the shelves.
9 Switch on again, or turn the thermostat control to the required number.
10 Replace the food.

rice

Rice goes well with so many dishes – stir-fries, curries, casseroles, and so on – that it's worth learning how to cook it. Different kinds of rice are distinguished by the size of the grain, and sometimes by their place of origin, for example Patna. Long grain rice is the type to buy to go with curries, etc. The small, round short grain rice is used for puddings.

A large packet of the supermarket's own brand long grain Patna rice is the most economical buy; it will keep for ages in a glass jar or plastic container. You will also find packets of 'Easy-Cook' rice – but it's not really any easier to cook and it works out considerably more expensive. White rice has been refined and does not contain as many nutrients as brown rice, which takes longer to cook. You need about 100g/4oz/²/₃ cup rice (which, if you don't have scales for measuring, is about 1 small cup) for one decent-sized serving.

to boil rice

Method 1
This is an absolutely foolproof way of cooking rice, that guarantees no more sticky messes.

1 Bring to the boil a large saucepan of water – you can speed this up by heating the water in a kettle first.
2 When the water is boiling add the rice and ¹/₂ teaspoon salt.
3 Bring back to the boil, and then lower the heat a little so that the rice is boiling fairly rapidly but without sloshing over the edges of the pan.
4 Boil for 12–15 minutes (25–30 minutes if using brown rice) until the rice is soft. To test if the rice is cooked squeeze a grain between your thumb and forefinger. If it is not properly cooked there will be

a hard particle of starch in the centre of each grain. When cooked it will be quite soft.

5 Drain the cooked rice into a sieve and rinse under hot water to remove excess starch and separate the grains.

6 Put about 1cm/½in water in the bottom of the saucepan, bring it to the boil and then reduce the heat so that the water continues to steam.

7 Rest the sieve containing the rice on top of the saucepan and steam it for 10 minutes – by which time the rice will be nice and fluffy, with the grains separated.

Method 2

I have never found this method of cooking rice as successful as Method 1, but some people swear by it. The important thing to remember is that the ratio of water to rice is 2:1.

1 Measure two small cups of water into a saucepan and bring it to the boil.

2 Add one small cup of rice and ½ teaspoon of salt.

3 Bring back to the boil, then reduce the heat to the lowest possible setting, cover the pan with a lid and simmer for 20 minutes (40 minutes if using brown rice).

4 Turn off the heat and leave for 5–10 minutes without lifting the lid.

spiced rice

Servings: 1
Time to prepare: 20–25 minutes

Sometimes you want something a little tastier than plain boiled rice. This spiced rice goes particularly well with kebabs and other skewered food. Rinse the rice thoroughly before cooking it to remove excess starch.

Ingredients	Metric	Imperial	American
water	*2 cups*	*2 cups*	*2 cups*
rice	*1 cup*	*1 cup*	*1 cup*
cloves	*3*	*3*	*3*
cinnamon stick	*1*	*1*	*1*
a pinch of turmeric			
salt	*¹/₂ tsp*	*¹/₂ tsp*	*¹/₂ tsp*
black pepper			

Equipment
Sieve, saucepan

Cooking method
Top of stove

1 Put the rice into a sieve and rinse it thoroughly under cold water until the water runs clear.
2 Bring the water to the boil in a saucepan.
3 Add the washed rice, cloves, cinnamon, turmeric, salt and a sprinkling of black pepper.
4 Reduce the heat a little so that the liquid is simmering gently.
5 Simmer for 12–15 minutes, until all the water has been absorbed and the rice is soft.

chicken pilaff

Servings: 1
Time to prepare: 20–25 minutes

Ingredients	Metric	Imperial	American
boiling water	*2 cups*	*2 cups*	*2 cups*
chicken stock (bouillon) cube	*1*	*1*	*1*
oil or butter	*1 tbsp*	*1 tbsp*	*1 tbsp*
small onion, peeled and finely chopped	*1*	*1*	*1*
cooked chicken, cut into strips			
rice	*1 cup*	*1 cup*	*1 cup*
tomato, chopped	*1*	*1*	*1*
dried thyme	*¼ tsp*	*¼ tsp*	*¼ tsp*
salt and pepper			

Equipment
Sieve, chopping board, sharp knife, saucepan

Cooking method
Top of stove

1 Put the rice into a sieve and rinse it thoroughly under cold water until the water runs clear. Leave to drain.
2 Heat the oil or butter in a saucepan.
3 Gently fry the onion until it is transparent.
4 Add the cooked chicken and fry until it is light brown.
5 Add the rice and continue cooking for 3 minutes, stirring continuously to stop it sticking to the pan.
6 Add the tomato, chicken stock, thyme, salt and pepper.
7 Bring to the boil, then reduce the heat until the liquid is simmering gently.

8 Simmer for 12–15 minutes, until all the water has been absorbed and the rice is soft.

9 Serve with peas or a green salad.

ham risotto

Servings: 1
Time to prepare: 20–25 minutes

The difference between a pilaff and a risotto is that in a pilaff the rice is dry, but in a real Italian risotto it is rich and creamy. Ideally a risotto should be made with short-grain Italian rice, but it is perfectly all right to use long-grain instead – even if the end result isn't quite as authentic.

Ingredients

Ingredients	Metric	Imperial	American
rice (Italian risotto rice or long grain)	*1 cup*	*1 cup*	*1 cup*
boiling water	*2 cups*	*2 cups*	*2 cups*
stock (bouillon) cube	*1*	*1*	*1*
oil	*1 tbsp*	*1 tbsp*	*1 tbsp*
small onion, peeled and chopped	*1*	*1*	*1*
green (bell) pepper, thinly sliced	*1/2*	*1/2*	*1/2*
thick slice of cooked ham, cut into thin strips or dice	*1*	*1*	*1*
tomato	*1*	*1*	*1*
salt and pepper			
grated Cheddar cheese	*1 tbsp*	*1 tbsp*	*1 tbsp*

Equipment
Sieve, chopping board, sharp knife, saucepan

Cooking method
Top of stove

1 Put the rice into a sieve and rinse it thoroughly under cold water until the water runs clear. Leave to drain.

2 Dissolve the stock (bouillon) cube in the boiling water.

3 Heat the oil in a saucepan.

4 Fry the onion and green pepper until they are soft.

5 Add the ham and fry gently for another 2 minutes.

6 Add the drained rice and cook, stirring continuously, for another 2 minutes.

7 Add the tomato and stir in the stock.

8 Season with salt and pepper.

9 Bring to the boil and then reduce the heat until the liquid is simmering gently.

10 Simmer for 12–15 minutes, until all the liquid is absorbed and the rice is soft.

11 Before eating sprinkle on the grated cheese.

12 Serve with a green salad.

ideas for using up cooked rice

Any left-over boiled rice can form the basis of another meal, so it's often worth cooking double the amount. (See cheesy rice (page 53) and rice salad (page 143).

● *for a really filling omelette, fry some chopped onion, add leftover rice, then stir in a tablespoon of grated cheese. Pour over a couple of beaten eggs. Cook until the base is set and then put under a hot grill to brown the top.*

fried rice

Servings: 1
Time to prepare: 15 minutes

You can add or substitute other ingredients to this basic recipe, according to what you have available.

Ingredients	Metric	Imperial	American
mug of cooked rice	*1*	*1*	*1*
rashers (slices) of bacon, cut into small pieces	*2*	*2*	*2*
oil	*1 tbsp*	*1 tbsp*	*1 tbsp*
small onion or 1 spring onion (scallion), finely chopped	*¹/₂*	*¹/₂*	*¹/₂*
button mushrooms, sliced	*2–3*	*2–3*	*2–3*
cooked peas or sweetcorn (corn kernels)	*1 tbsp*	*1 tbsp*	*1 tbsp*
salt and pepper			

Equipment
Frying pan (skillet), chopping board, sharp knife

Cooking method
Top of stove

1 Heat the frying pan (skillet) on a medium heat and fry the bacon for 2–3 minutes.
2 Add the oil and fry the onion and mushrooms gently for 3 minutes.
3 Add the cooked rice and peas or sweetcorn.
4 Continue frying for 4–5 minutes, stirring all the time, until everything is heated through.
5 Season with salt and pepper.

the **S** s

salads

Salads can be made from a great variety of vegetables, both raw and cooked, and with fruit, nuts and herbs to give flavour and colour. Add meat, fish, egg or cheese – either hot or cold – to make a complete meal. Salads are very easy to prepare – the ones given here take only a few minutes to assemble – and there's endless variety. Once you've tried some of these and invented more of your own you will never want to see a limp lettuce leaf again.

to make French dressing

You will find a huge variety of commercially-prepared salad dressings in the supermarket, but it is very easy, and much cheaper, to make your own.

In a small screw-top jar mix together 2 tablespoons sunflower oil (or olive oil if you can afford it), 1 tablespoon vinegar (preferably wine vinegar, malt vinegar is too strong), ¼ teaspoon caster (superfine) sugar, a pinch of dry mustard, salt and pepper. Shake well before using. French dressing keeps all right if you make more than you need.

● *The following recipes all serve one person. The only equipment necessary is a chopping board, sharp knife, salad bowl and, in some cases, a grater.*

green salad

Ingredients	Metric	Imperial	American
Several leaves from a selection of green salad plants, such as lettuce, cress, watercress, endive, chicory and sorrel			
clove of garlic	*1*	*1*	*1*
French dressing	*1 tbsp*	*1 tbsp*	*1 tbsp*
fresh chopped herbs,such as basil, parsley or chervil	*1 tsp*	*1 tsp*	*1 tsp*

1 Wash the salad in cold water and shake dry.
2 Slice or shred the leaves.
3 Rub a serving bowl with garlic to add extra flavour before putting in the salad.
4 Pour over the French dressing and toss the salad well.
5 Sprinkle on the chopped herbs.

carrot salad

Ingredients	Metric	Imperial	American
large carrot	1	1	1
small onion	$^1/_2$	$^1/_2$	$^1/_2$
French dressing	1 tbsp	1 tbsp	1 tbsp

1 Grate the carrot and onion.
2 Mix well with the French dressing.

celery and apple salad

Ingredients	Metric	Imperial	American
sticks (stalks) of celery	2	2	2
red eating apple	1	1	1
currants	2 tsp	2 tsp	2 tsp
a few walnut halves			
French dressing	1 tbsp	1 tbsp	1 tbsp

1 Slice the celery into small pieces.
2 Quarter the apple, remove the core and cut into thin slices.
3 Put celery, apple, currants and walnut halves into a serving bowl.
4 Toss well in French dressing.

tomato salad

Ingredients	Metric	Imperial	American
tomatoes	2	2	2
small onion	1	1	1
French dressing	1 tbsp	1 tbsp	1 tbsp

1 Slice the tomatoes and onion thinly and place in layers in a bowl.
2 Spoon the French dressing over the salad and leave for an hour before eating.

salade niçoise

Ingredients	Metric	Imperial	American
small tin tuna fish in brine	1	1	1
lettuce leaves	2–3	2–3	2–3
tomato, sliced	1	1	1
black (ripe) olives	6	6	6
anchovies (keep the rest of the tin for anchovy toast)	3–4	3–4	3–4
green (bell) pepper, thinly sliced	1/2	1/2	1/2
French dressing	1 tbsp	1 tbsp	1 tbsp

1 Wash the lettuce leaves and shake dry.
2 Lay the leaves in a dish, then arrange the tuna fish, tomato, olives, anchovies, and green pepper on top.
3 Sprinkle over the French dressing.

tuna coleslaw

Ingredients	Metric	Imperial	American
small tin tuna fish in brine	1	1	1
small white cabbage	¼	¼	¼
chopped pineapple	1 tbsp	1 tbsp	1 tbsp
tomato	1	1	1
French dressing	1 tbsp	1 tbsp	1 tbsp
anchovy fillets	3–4	3–4	3–4

1 Shred the cabbage as finely as possible.
2 Mix with the chopped pineapple and French dressing – this should be done half an hour before serving.
3 Arrange slices of tomato on top.
4 Drain and flake the tuna and spoon into the middle of the salad.
5 Place the anchovy fillets on top of the tuna.

egg mayonnaise

Ingredients	Metric	Imperial	American
hard-boiled egg	1	1	1
mayonnaise	1 tbsp	1 tbsp	1 tbsp
lettuce leaves	2	2	2
paprika			

1 Arrange the lettuce leaves on a small plate.
2 Cut the egg in half lengthways and place cut side down on the lettuce.
3 Spoon the mayonnaise over the egg.
4 Sprinkle with a little paprika.

● *When cooking rice, cook a little extra to make rice salad for your next meal. Use while still hot, to absorb the flavours of the French dressing.*

rice salad

Ingredients	Metric	Imperial	American
cooked rice, still hot	2–3 tbsp	2–3 tbsp	2–3 tbsp
French dressing	1 tbsp	1 tbsp	1 tbsp
spring onion (scallion)	1	1	1
small stalk celery	1	1	1
small green (bell) pepper	$^1/_2$	$^1/_2$	$^1/_2$
a few salted peanuts or cashew nuts			
salt and pepper			

1 To the hot rice, add the French dressing and mix thoroughly so that all the grains are covered.
2 Finely chop the spring onion (scallion), celery and green pepper and add to the rice with the nuts.
3 Season with salt and pepper.
4 Leave to cool.

• *When cooking pasta shapes, cook a little extra to make pasta salad for your next meal. Refresh the pasta in cold water before mixing into the salad.*

pasta salad

Ingredients	Metric	Imperial	American
cooked pasta shapes – shells or spirals	1 cup	1 cup	1 cup
spring onions (scallions), chopped	2	2	2
small carrot, grated	1	1	1
a few green beans, cooked and cooled			
small red or green (bell) pepper, diced			
lettuce leaves	2–3	2–3	2–3
French dressing	1 tbsp	1 tbsp	1 tbsp

1 Wash the lettuce leaves and shake dry.
2 Combine all the other ingredients and mix with French dressing.
3 Arrange the lettuce leaves in a dish and pile the other ingredients on top.

● *When cooking new potatoes, put in a few extra to make potato salad for your next meal. Use the potatoes while they are still hot so that they absorb the flavours of the mayonnaise and vinegar.*

potato salad

Ingredients	Metric	Imperial	American
new potatoes, still hot	6	6	6
spring onions (scallions)	1–2	1–2	1–2
mayonnaise	1 tbsp	1 tbsp	1 tbsp
vinegar	2 tsp	2 tsp	2 tsp
salt and pepper			

1 Cut the potatoes into neat cubes while they are still hot.
2 Chop the spring onions (scallions).
3 Mix potato and onion with the mayonnaise and vinegar.
4 Season with salt and pepper and leave to cool.

sausages

Some people eat them all the time because they are the only food they can cook; others avoid them because they worry about what is inside. If you fall somewhere between these two categories, here are some ideas for meals with sausages.

Generally speaking, the more you pay for your sausages the higher the meat content. They can be made from any meat, though pork and beef are the most popular. Like meat, they are very perishable and should be cooked within a couple of days of purchase.

grilling (broiling)

Have the grill (broiler) on medium heat. Prick the skin of the sausages with a fork to stop them bursting during cooking. Put them on the grid in the grill pan and cook for 10–15 minutes, turning occasionally so that they brown evenly on all sides. For bangers and mash, mix some instant mashed potato to go with the sausages, or follow the instructions on page 120.

frying

Heat a little oil in a frying pan (skillet) and fry the sausages on medium heat for 10–15 minutes, turning occasionally so that they brown evenly on all sides. If you like them, fry sliced onions alongside.

sausage hotpot

Servings: 1
Time to prepare: 1 hour 10 minutes

Ingredients	Metric	Imperial	American
sausages	*3–4*	*3–4*	*3–4*
small onion, peeled and sliced	*1*	*1*	*1*
carrot, peeled and sliced	*1*	*1*	*1*
potatoes, peeled and sliced	*2*	*2*	*2*
packet soup mix	*¹/₂*	*¹/₂*	*¹/₂*
salt and pepper			

Equipment
Ovenproof dish with lid, chopping board, sharp knife

Cooking method
Oven

1 Turn on the oven, set at 375°F/190°C Gas Mark 5.
2 Put the sausages, sliced onion and carrot into an ovenproof dish.
3 Arrange slices of potato on top.
4 Mix the packet soup with a cup of water and pour over the top.
5 Add salt and pepper.
6 Put on the lid and cook in the oven for 1 hour. (Remove the lid 15 minutes before the end of cooking time to crisp the potatoes on top.)

frankfurters

These sausages are already cooked. Heat them in gently simmering water for 10–15 minutes, but do not boil or they will split. Frankfurters go well with sauerkraut (which you can buy in tins) beans, and jacket potatoes. Or you could make a hot-dog by putting a hot frankfurter inside a roll – with some fried onions and/or mustard and tomato ketchup if you like them.

cooked, ready-to-eat sausages

The delicatessen counter of the supermarket will have a selection of cooked sausages to eat cold with salads, in sandwiches, etc. There are many different types of salami, which come from all over the world. Others to look out for are garlic sausage, and mortadella – a very large Italian sausage made from pork, garlic, and coriander seeds.

seasoning

Seasoning means adding salt, pepper, herbs or spices to food. Without at least a little seasoning food would taste pretty awful – and some dishes rely on particular herbs or spices for their distinctive flavour.

Many of the recipes in this book include 'season with salt and pepper. How much of these you add to the dish is a matter of personal taste and trial and error. The advice these days is to try and cut down on the amount of salt in our food, and you can usually compensate for the loss of flavour by adding other herbs and spices. A 'pinch' of salt is the amount you can pick up between your thumb and forefinger.

herbs

You can buy the most common herbs fresh in health food shops and some supermarkets, and they will stay fresh for a few days if you put them in a plastic bag in the salad drawer of the refrigerator. It is more convenient to buy dried ones, which will keep for 6–9 months in a glass jar with an airtight seal. Store them away from light and heat. At the very least, have a jar of mixed herbs in your store cupboard. Half a teaspoonful added to a casserole or sprinkled on top of a pizza makes all the difference to the taste.

spices

Spices are the dried, aromatic parts of certain plants – usually the seeds, pods, berries, roots, stems or buds. You can buy them whole or ground. Whole spices can be crushed or ground with a pestle and mortar. Ground spices are much easier to use, but they lose their flavour, scent and colour more quickly, so it is better not to keep them for more than six months. Keep in airtight glass jars away from heat and light.

slow cooking

Heating a whole oven to cook just one portion of food is uneconomical because it uses a lot of gas or electricity. A useful piece of equipment, particularly if your cooking facilities are limited, is a slow-cooker. This is an electric casserole, consisting of a glazed earthenware pot in an outer casing of aluminium or heat-resistant plastic. It is heated by elements between the pot and the outer casing, and uses very little electricity because it cooks at a very low temperature.

The disadvantage of the slow-cooker is that you need to be organised – you have to put all the ingredients in some hours ahead and leave them cooking. But the advantage is that you can then go out and return to find a tasty meal waiting for you – and it doesn't spoil if you are an hour or two late. A slow cooker is ideal for cheaper cuts of meat because the long cooking time breaks down the tough texture and improves the flavour. It is also useful for recipes containing pulses. A compact slow-cooker that holds about 1.5 ltrs/2¾pts/7 cups is more than big enough for one person.

Any of the recipes in the Casseroles Section of this book can also be cooked in a slow cooker.

reheating

To save time and energy (yours as well as the electricity) it's a good idea to cook enough for two meals. The second portion can either be heated up the next day or put into a foil container and kept in the freezer compartment of the refrigerator until you want it. To reheat, place the covered dish (thaw it first if frozen) in the slow-cooker and pour boiling water round it. Heat on low for 1–2 hours, depending on the quantity.

beef casserole

Servings: 2
Cooking time: 7–10 hours

Ingredients	Metric	Imperial	American
stewing beef, cut into cubes	275g	10oz	10oz
oil	1 tbsp	1 tbsp	1 tbsp
onion, peeled and sliced	1	1	1
stick of celery, chopped	1	1	1
carrots, thinly sliced	2	2	2
large potatoes, cut into 1cm/¹/₂ cubes	2	2	2
flour	2 tsp	2 tsp	2 tsp
beef stock (made with a stock (bouillon) cube)	300ml	¹/₂pt	1¹/₄ cups
tomato purée (paste)	2 tsp	2 tsp	2 tsp
dried mixed herbs	¹/₂ tsp	¹/₂ tsp	¹/₂ tsp
salt and pepper			

Equipment
Saucepan, fish slice (pancake turner) or slotted spoon, chopping board, sharp knife, small basin

Cooking method
Slow cooker

1 Heat the oil in a saucepan and fry the meat until it is lightly browned all over.
2 Lift out the meat with a fish slice (pancake turner) or slotted spoon and transfer it to the slow cooker.
3 In the same oil fry the vegetables gently for 5 minutes.
4 In a small basin, mix the flour with a little of the beef stock to make a smooth paste.

5 Stir in the rest of the stock, then pour it over the vegetables.
6 Add the tomato purée (paste) and herbs, and season with salt and pepper.
7 Bring to the boil, then transfer the mixture to the slow cooker.
8 Cook for 7–10 hours.

paella

Servings: 1
Cooking time: 3–4 hours

Ingredients	Metric	Imperial	American
oil	1 tbsp	1 tbsp	1 tbsp
small onion, peeled and sliced	1	1	1
clove of garlic, crushed	1	1	1
red (bell) pepper, deseeded and finely chopped	1/2	1/2	1/2
long grain rice	1 cup	1 cup	1 cup
chicken stock, made with a stock (bouillon) cube	2 cups	2 cups	2 cups
a pinch of turmeric			
tomato, chopped	1	1	1
cooked chicken, chopped			
small tin smoked mussels	1	1	1
prawns (shrimp)	100g	4oz	2/3 cup
peas, frozen or tinned	1/2 cup	1/2 cup	1/2 cup
salt and pepper			

Equipment
Sieve, saucepan, chopping board, sharp knife

Cooking method
Slow cooker

1 Put the rice into a sieve and rinse thoroughly under cold water until the water runs clear.
2 Heat the oil in a saucepan and fry the onion and garlic gently for 3 minutes.
3 Add the red pepper and continue frying for another 2 minutes.
4 Add the chicken stock and turmeric and bring to the boil.
5 Add the tomato, chicken and mussels, and season with salt and pepper.
6 Bring to the boil again and transfer to the slow cooker.
7 Cook on low for 3–4 hours.
8 30 minutes before the end of cooking time, stir in the prawn (shrimp) and peas.

soup

A hearty soup provides a satisfying meal at any time of the year, especially if you eat it with a hunk of fresh crusty bread and some cheese. It is easy to make your own, and this will taste ten times better and cost less than anything that comes out of a tin. Always make enough for more than one serving, because soup will keep for several days in the fridge. Make sure you bring it to the boil each time you reheat it.

frankfurter soup

Servings: 2
Time to prepare: 50 minutes

Ingredients	Metric	Imperial	American
butter or margarine	1 tbsp	1 tbsp	1 tbsp
small onion, peeled and chopped	1	1	1
leek, washed and sliced	1	1	1
potatoes, peeled and diced	2	2	2
chicken stock, made with a chicken stock (bouillon) cube	450ml	³/₄pt	2 cups
coriander seeds, or ground coriander	¹/₄ tsp	¹/₄ tsp	¹/₄ tsp
salt and pepper			
milk	150ml	¹/₄ pt	²/₃ cup
frankfurter sausages, sliced	2	2	2

Equipment
Saucepan, chopping board, sharp knife

Cooking method
Top of stove

1 Melt the butter in a saucepan and gently fry the onion and leek for 5 minutes.
2 Add the diced potato, chicken stock and seasoning.
3 Bring to the boil, then reduce the heat, cover with a lid and simmer for 30 minutes.
4 Add the milk and frankfurters and continue simmering for another 10 minutes.

minestrone soup

Servings: 2
Time to prepare: 40 minutes

Ingredients	Metric	Imperial	American
small carrot, diced	1	1	1
leek, washed and sliced	1	1	1
small onion, peeled and sliced	1	1	1
courgette (zucchini), washed and diced	1	1	1
stick of celery, washed and sliced	1	1	1
clove of garlic, peeled and crushed	1	1	1
oil	1 tbsp	1 tbsp	1 tbsp
stock, made with a stock (bouillon) cube	600ml	1 pint	2¹/₂ cups
salt and pepper			
dried mixed herbs	¹/₂ tsp	¹/₂ tsp	¹/₂ tsp
tomato	1	1	1
frozen peas	1 tbsp	1 tbsp	1 tbsp
small pasta shapes	1 tbsp	1 tbsp	1 tbsp
tomato purée (paste)	1 tsp	1 tsp	1 tsp
Parmesan cheese			

Equipment
Saucepan, chopping board, sharp knife

Cooking method
Top of stove

1 Heat the oil in a saucepan and add the carrot, leek, onion, courgette (zucchini), celery, and garlic. Cook gently for 5 minutes.
2 Add the stock, herbs, salt and pepper.

3 Bring to the boil, then reduce the heat, cover with a lid and simmer for 20 minutes.
4 Add the tomato, peas, pasta shapes and tomato purée (paste).
5 Cook for a further 10 minutes.
6 Serve with grated Parmesan cheese sprinkled on top.

potato and onion soup

Servings: 1
Time to prepare: 20–25 minutes

Ingredients	Metric	Imperial	American
large onion, peeled and sliced	1	1	1
large potato, peeled and cut into pieces	1	1	1
carrot	1	1	1
milk	300ml	½pt	1¼ cups
salt and pepper			
grated Cheddar cheese	1 tbsp	1 tbsp	1 tbsp

Equipment
Small saucepan, chopping board, sharp knife, grater

Cooking method
Top of stove

1 Put the vegetables into a small saucepan and just cover them with water.
2 Bring to the boil, then reduce the heat, cover with a lid and simmer for 15 minutes, until the potatoes are soft.
3 Break the vegetables down a little with a fork (but do not mash them) and add the milk.
4 Season with salt and pepper.
5 Bring back to the boil.
6 Sprinkle the grated cheese on top before eating.

stews

Stews are basically the same as casseroles – a mixture of meat and vegetables cooked slowly together. The differences are that stews are cooked in a saucepan on top of the stove, and more liquid is required.

As with casseroles, the cheaper, tougher cuts of meat are ideal, and it is a good idea to cook enough for at least two meals because a stew tastes even better reheated. When reheating, the stew **must** be brought to the boil and simmered for 20 minutes.

Suitable ingredients for stews are the same as for Casseroles (see page 42).

basic method for cooking stews

1 Cut up the meat; peel and slice the vegetables; make stock by dissolving a stock (bouillon) cube in boiling water.
2 Melt some fat in a saucepan and when it is really hot add the meat and sliced onion. Fry quickly, stirring all the time, until the meat is brown on all sides.
3 Sprinkle a tablespoon of flour over the meat, stir, and cook for another minute.
4 Gradually add stock, stirring all the time to stop lumps forming.
5 Add the vegetables, herbs if you are using them, salt and pepper.
6 Bring to the boil, then reduce the heat, cover with a lid and simmer for 1½–2 hours, or until the meat is tender.

beef stew with dumplings

Servings: 2
Time to prepare: 2 hours

The dumplings in this recipe won't stand reheating –
make some fresh ones for the second serving.

Ingredients	Metric	Imperial	American
stewing or braising steak, cut into cubes	*225–275g*	*8–10oz*	*8–10oz*
onion, peeled and sliced	*1*	*1*	*1*
oil	*1 tbsp*	*1 tbsp*	*1 tbsp*
flour	*1 tbsp*	*1 tbsp*	*1 tbsp*
stock, made with a beef stock (bouillon) cube	*450ml*	*³/₄pt*	*2 cups*
carrot, sliced	*1*	*1*	*1*
small parsnip, peeled and chopped	*1*	*1*	*1*
small turnip, peeled and chopped	*1*	*1*	*1*
tomato purée (paste)	*2 tsp*	*2 tsp*	*2 tsp*
a dash of Worcestershire sauce			
salt and pepper			

For the dumplings

self-raising flour	*2 tbsp*	*2 tbsp*	*2 tbsp*
shredded suet	*1 tbsp*	*1 tbsp*	*1 tbsp*
a pinch of salt			
mixed dried herbs	*¹/₂ tsp*	*¹/₂ tsp*	*¹/₂ tsp*
water			

Equipment
Large saucepan with lid, chopping board, sharp knife,
small mixing bowl

Cooking method
Top of stove

1 Heat the oil in a saucepan and when it is really hot add the meat and sliced onion.
2 Fry quickly, stirring all the time, until the meat is brown on all sides.
3 Sprinkle over the flour and continue cooking for another minute.
4 Gradually add the stock, stirring all the time to prevent lumps forming.
5 Add the vegetables, tomato purée (paste), and Worcestershire sauce.
6 Season with salt and pepper.
7 Bring to the boil, then reduce the heat and cover with a lid.
8 Simmer for $1^{1}/_{2}$–$1^{3}/_{4}$ hours.
9 Meanwhile, make the dumplings. Put all the ingredients into a small mixing bowl and add just enough cold water to make a soft dough.
10 Divide the dough into 3 portions and roll each into a little ball.
11 Check that the meat in the stew is just about tender, then add the dumplings.
12 Cook for another 15–20 minutes, until the dumplings have swelled up and are light and fluffy.

Irish stew

Servings: 2
Time to prepare: $2^{1}/_{2}$ hours

Dumplings would go well with this lamb stew – see the instructions above for making them.

Ingredients

	Metric	Imperial	American
middle neck or scrag end of lamb (blade or arm chops)	350–450g	12oz–1lb	3/4–1lb
oil	1 tbsp	1 tbsp	1 tbsp
large onion, peeled and sliced	1	1	1
carrots, sliced	2	2	2
potatoes, peeled and cut into chunks	2	2	2
stock, made with a stock (bouillon) cube	450ml	3/4pt	2 cups
salt and pepper			
mixed dried herbs	1/2 tsp	1/2 tsp	1/2 tsp

Equipment
Large saucepan with lid, chopping board, sharp knife

Cooking method
Top of stove

1 Cut any surplus fat off the meat.
2 Heat the oil in a saucepan and when it is really hot add the meat and onion.
3 Fry until the meat is browned on all sides.
4 Add the carrots and potatoes and fry for another 2 minutes, stirring all the time to stop them sticking to the pan.
5 Add the stock, herbs, salt and pepper.
6 Bring to the boil, then reduce the heat and cover with a lid.
7 Simmer for about 2–2½ hours, until the meat is tender.
8 If you are making dumplings, add them about 20 minutes before the end of cooking time.

stir-fry

Stir-frying is a quick and easy way of cooking that is ideal if you are making a meal just for one. It is based on the Chinese way of preparing food – vegetables and meat are chopped up into small pieces and cooked in a small amount of oil over a very high heat, and you have to stir all the time to prevent them sticking or burning.

Because stir-fry dishes are cooked very quickly you have to use tender, good quality meat like good steak or chicken breasts – but you don't need much of it. If you have time it is a good idea to leave the meat to soak (marinate) for half an hour or longer in some soy sauce, or wine vinegar – this makes it more tender. Most vegetables are suitable. The trick is to have all the ingredients prepared – sliced, chopped or grated – and lined up in the order you are going to use them before you start the actual cooking. It's no good searching in the back of the cupboard for the soy sauce while the food is burning on the stove.

A wok is ideal for cooking stir-fry dishes, but if you don't have one a large non-stick frying pan (skillet) will do. You will also need a really sharp knife and a chopping board as there is a lot of slicing and chopping involved. Stir-fried meat and vegetables are usually served with rice or noodles, so you will also need a large saucepan to cook these in. (See the Rice Section for how to cook rice.)

Some of the ingredients in the following recipes may sound unfamiliar, but they can all be bought in a good supermarket. There is now quite a wide range of sauces to mix into stir-fried food – things like sweet and sour sauce, oyster sauce, black bean, yellow bean – and these are simplicity itself to use. You probably won't use a whole jar for just one person, but you can store the remainder in the refrigerator.

If you are likely to cook stir-fry dishes fairly often, it's a good idea to keep a few basics in the store cupboard – rice, noodles, soy sauce, sesame oil, for example.

beef and green pepper in oyster sauce

Servings: 1
Time to prepare: 20 minutes

This works equally well with black bean sauce – which has a spicier flavour.

Ingredients	Metric	Imperial	American
long grain rice	1 cup	1 cup	1 cup
steak (frying, rump or sirloin – it must be tender)	100g	4oz	4oz
green (bell) pepper	1	1	1
cooking oil	1 tbsp	1 tbsp	1 tbsp
oyster sauce	3 tbsp	3 tbsp	3 tbsp

Equipment
Frying pan (skillet) or wok, saucepan, sieve, wooden spoon, chopping board, knife

Cooking method
Top of stove

1 See page 131 for cooking rice.
2 While the rice is cooking, cut the steak across the grain into thin slices.
3 Remove the stalk and seeds from the pepper and slice thinly.
4 Heat the oil in the frying pan (skillet) or wok.
5 When the oil is really hot add the sliced meat and cook for 3 minutes, stirring all the time.

6 Add the sliced pepper and continue cooking for 2 more minutes.
7 Turn down the heat and add the oyster sauce.
8 Heat through gently for 5 minutes, while the rice is steaming.
9 Serve on a bed of rice.

sweet and sour pork

Servings: 1
Time to prepare: 25 minutes

The easiest way to make this dish is to buy a jar of ready-made sweet and sour sauce and pour it over the stir-fried pork according to the instructions on the label. The following method takes more effort. You could use chicken in this recipe instead of pork.

Ingredients	Metric	Imperial	American
long grain rice	1 cup	1 cup	1 cup
lean pork, fillet (tenderloin) or a pork steak	100g	4oz	4oz
vinegar	1 tbsp	1 tbsp	1 tbsp
soy sauce	1 tbsp	1 tbsp	1 tbsp
onion, finely chopped	1/2	1/2	1/2
green (bell) pepper, chopped	1/2	1/2	1/2
carrot, finely chopped	1	1	1
oil	1 tbsp	1 tbsp	1 tbsp
sugar	1 tsp	1 tsp	1 tsp
tomato purée (paste)	1 tsp	1 tsp	1 tsp
pineapple juice	2 tbsp	2 tbsp	2 tbsp
cornflour (corn starch), mixed with a little water	1 tsp	1 tsp	1 tsp
salt and pepper			

Equipment
Frying pan (skillet) or wok, basin, saucepan, sieve, wooden spoon, chopping board, knife, fish slice (pancake turner) or slotted spoon

Cooking method
Top of stove

1 Cut the pork into small cubes and put into a small basin.
2 Mix thoroughly with the vinegar and soy sauce until all the meat is coated and leave to marinate.
3 Meanwhile cook the rice (see page 131) and prepare the vegetables.
4 When you are ready to stir-fry, lift the meat from the marinade sauce with a slotted spoon or fish slice (pancake turner).
5 Stir the sugar, tomato purée (paste), pineapple juice and cornflour (corn starch) mixed with a little water into the sauce left in the basin.
6 Heat the oil in the frying pan (skillet) or wok.
7 When the oil is really hot add the pork and cook, stirring all the time, for 3 minutes.
8 Add the vegetables and continue cooking and stirring for 2 more minutes.
9 Pour over the sauce and bring it to the boil.
10 Simmer for a couple of minutes.
11 Serve on a bed of rice.

chicken chow mein

Servings: 1
Time to prepare: 20 minutes

Ingredients	Metric	Imperial	American
packet medium egg noodles	1/2	1/2	1/2
skinned and boned chicken	100g	4oz	1/2 cup
small onion	1	1	1
clove of garlic	1	1	1
carrot	1	1	1
fresh beansprouts (or a tin)	150g	6oz	3 cups
oil	1 tbsp	1 tbsp	1 tbsp
light soy sauce	1 tbsp	1 tbsp	1 tbsp
sesame oil	1 tsp	1 tsp	1 tsp
sugar	1/2 tsp	1/2 tsp	1/2 tsp
a pinch of salt			

Equipment
Frying pan (skillet) or wok, large saucepan, sieve, wooden spoon, chopping board, knife, grater

Cooking method
Top of stove

1 Slice the chicken thinly to match the shape of the noodles.
2 Peel and thinly slice the onion and garlic.
3 Peel or scrape the carrot and grate it.
4 Put the noodles into a saucepan of boiling water, remove from the heat and cover with the lid. Put on one side.
5 Meanwhile heat the oil in the frying pan (skillet) or wok.
6 When it is hot add the sliced chicken and cook for 3 minutes, stirring all the time with the wooden spoon.

7 Add the sliced onion, garlic and grated carrot, and stir-fry for another 2 minutes.
8 Add the bean sprouts, soy sauce, sesame oil, sugar and salt, and mix all the ingredients together.
9 Turn off the heat.
10 The noodles will now be cooked – empty them through the sieve and make sure they drain properly.
11 If the wok or frying pan is large enough, add the noodles to the other ingredients – if not, put everything into the large saucepan.
12 Mix everything together thoroughly and heat gently for a few minutes before serving.

egg fried rice

Servings: 1
Time to prepare: 10 minutes

This is an excellent way of using up cooked rice. If you have to cook it from scratch, add another 15 minutes to the preparation time.

Ingredients	Metric	Imperial	American
cooked rice	*1 cup*	*1 cup*	*1 cup*
egg	*1*	*1*	*1*
vegetable oil	*2 tsp*	*2 tsp*	*2 tsp*
small clove of garlic, finely chopped	*1*	*1*	*1*
spring onions (scallions), finely chopped	*2*	*2*	*2*
peas, frozen or tinned	*1/2 cup*	*1/2 cup*	*1/2 cup*
light soy sauce	*2 tsp*	*2 tsp*	*2 tsp*
salt			

Equipment
Bowl, small saucepan, frying pan (skillet)

Cooking method
Top of stove

1 Break the egg into a bowl and beat it well with a fork.
2 Pour into a small saucepan and cook gently on a low heat, stirring until lightly scrambled.
3 Put the scrambled egg to one side and heat the oil in a frying pan (skillet).
4 Add the garlic, spring onions (scallions) and peas and stir-fry for 1 minute.
5 Stir in the cooked rice and mix thoroughly.
6 Add the soy sauce, scrambled egg and salt to taste.
7 Stir to break up the egg and mix thoroughly.

store cupboard

When you move into rented accommodation you will want at least the basic essentials – tea, coffee, milk, sugar, bread, margarine or butter, and perhaps some eggs and cheese – to see you through the first evening and breakfast the next morning. After that you will have to go food shopping. Perishable items like meat and vegetables need to be bought fairly regularly and kept in the refrigerator. Non-perishables such as rice and pulses are cheaper if you buy in bulk and store them in airtight jars or plastic containers. Empty coffee jars and margarine tubs make good storage receptacles.

Whether you go shopping every day or once a week will depend on how much time you have, how much storage space is available, whether you have the use of a refrigerator to keep things fresh – and whether you actually like shopping. The best place to shop is a large supermarket, where you will find everything you want under one roof, and the food is likely to be fresh. The supermarket's own-brand goods will be cheaper than named brands, and there will often be special offers. Late on Saturday afternoon is a good time to shop because perishable items are usually considerably reduced then.

Small corner shops often stay open late and are handy when you find you have run out of something or haven't had time to shop during the day. Most towns also have open-air markets, and these are usually good for fruit and vegetables, fish, and any local produce.

Storage space will almost certainly be a problem in your rented accommodation, but it is worth keeping a small stock of tins and other non-perishable items on a spare shelf or even in a cardboard box under the bed. These will provide you with a quick meal when you don't have time to shop.

Suggested items for your store cupboard

Baked beans
Butter (Lima or fava) beans (tinned or dried)
Chick peas (garbanzo beans) (tinned or dried)
Coffee
Curry powder (or individual spices)
Dried mixed herbs
Flour
Lemon juice (in a plastic container)
Lentils
Milk powder (for emergencies)
Mustard
Noodles
Oil (for cooking)
Parmesan cheese
Pasta shapes

Pepper
Pineapple cubes (for kebabs, stir-fries or dessert)
Red kidney beans (tinned or dried)
Rice
Rolled oats
Salt
Sardines
Soup (condensed in tins, and packet mixes
   for casseroles)
Soy sauce
Spaghetti
Stock (bouillon) cubes
Sugar
Sweetcorn (corn kernels)
Teabags
Tinned tomatoes
Tomato purée (paste)
Tomato sauce
Tuna fish
Vinegar
Worcestershire sauce

the T s

tea-time

Think of a cold winter's afternoon, and a group of hungry people huddled round your gas fire. Then imagine how their faces will light up when you produce some hot tea and a plate of home-made cakes or biscuits (cookies). All of the following recipes are easy and inexpensive.

Tea-bags are obviously more convenient than loose tea – they don't block the sink and you don't need a tea-pot. However, loose tea is cheaper and purists will say that it tastes much better.

There are now all kinds of herb teas available, which are said to be better for you because they don't contain caffeine. Certainly they make a refreshing or relaxing drink – experiment to find one that you really like. Honey is a good sweetener.

how to make a decent pot of tea

1 Throw away any leftover water in the kettle and fill with fresh cold water.
2 When the water is almost boiling, pour some into the teapot to warm it, then empty it out.
3 Put 1 level teaspoon of tea for each person, plus 'one for the pot', into the heated teapot.
4 As soon as the water boils, pour it on the tea.
5 Allow to stand and infuse for 3–5 minutes.
6 Stir the tea, then pour into cups through a strainer.
7 When the first cups have been poured, top up the teapot with some more boiling water, ready for second cups.

flapjacks

Makes: 10–12
Time to prepare: 30 minutes

Ingredients	Metric	Imperial	American
rolled oats	*1¹/₂ cups*	*1¹/₂ cups*	*1¹/₂ cups*
margarine or butter	*6 tbsp*	*6 tbsp*	*6 tbsp*
sugar	*6 tbsp*	*6 tbsp*	*6 tbsp*
golden (corn) syrup	*2 tbsp*	*2 tbsp*	*2 tbsp*

Equipment
Saucepan, shallow baking tin or ovenproof dish

Cooking method
Top of stove, then oven

1 Turn on the oven, set at 375°F/190°C Gas Mark 5.
2 Put the margarine, sugar and syrup into a saucepan and heat gently until the margarine has melted and the sugar dissolved.
3 Stir in the rolled oats.

4 Smear plenty of oil or margarine over the base and sides of a shallow baking tin or ovenproof dish.
5 Spoon the flapjack mixture into it, using the back of the spoon to spread the mixture out to completely cover the base.
6 Bake in the preheated oven for 15 minutes.
7 Leave the flapjack to cool a little, and then mark it into ten or twelve slices.
8 When it has completely cooked, cut the wedges out.

chocolate crispies

Makes: 12
Time to prepare: 15 minutes

Ingredients	Metric	Imperial	American
block margarine	2 tbsp	2 tbsp	2 tbsp
sugar	2 tbsp	2 tbsp	2 tbsp
golden (corn) syrup	2 tbsp	2 tbsp	2 tbsp
(unsweetened) cocoa powder	2 tbsp	2 tbsp	2 tbsp
cornflakes or rice crispies	3 cups	3 cups	3 cups

Equipment
Saucepan, paper cases

Cooking method
Top of stove

1 Put the margarine, sugar and syrup into a large saucepan and heat gently until the margarine has melted and sugar dissolved.
2 Stir in the cocoa powder.
3 Stir in the cornflakes or rice crispies, mixing well to coat them thoroughly with the chocolate mixture.
4 Put a couple of spoonfuls into each paper case and leave to set.

date chews

Makes: 12–16
Time to prepare: 55 minutes

Ingredients

	Metric	Imperial	American
plain flour	*6 tbsp*	*6 tbsp*	*6 tbsp*
desiccated (shredded) coconut	*3 tbsp*	*3 tbsp*	*3 tbsp*
chopped dates	*150g*	*6oz*	*³/₄ cup*
sugar	*6 tbsp*	*6 tbsp*	*6 tbsp*
margarine	*3 tbsp*	*3 tbsp*	*3 tbsp*
golden (corn) syrup	*2 tsp*	*2 tsp*	*2 tsp*
egg, beaten	*1*	*1*	*1*

Equipment
Mixing bowl, saucepan, shallow baking tin or oven-proof dish

Cooking method
Top of stove, then oven

1 Turn on the oven, set at 325°F/160°C Gas Mark 3.
2 Smear plenty of margarine over the base of a shallow baking tin or ovenproof dish.
3 Put the flour, coconut and dates into a mixing bowl.
4 Put the sugar, margarine and syrup into a saucepan and heat gently until the margarine has melted and the sugar dissolved.
5 Stir this mixture into the dry ingredients in the mixing bowl.
6 Stir in the beaten egg.
7 When well mixed, spoon the mixture into the baking tin, using the back of the spoon to press it well into the corners.
8 Bake for 40–45 minutes, until golden brown.
9 Cut into fingers or squares, and leave to cool.

biscuits

Makes: 10–12
Time to prepare: 30 minutes

These biscuits (cookies) can be varied by adding different ingredients to the basic mix. Or you can sprinkle things on top – such as grated chocolate, chopped nuts or coconut.

Ingredients	Metric	Imperial	American
soft brown sugar	*2 tbsp*	*2 tbsp*	*2 tbsp*
soft tub margarine	*2 tbsp*	*2 tbsp*	*2 tbsp*
egg, beaten	*¹/₂*	*¹/₂*	*¹/₂*
plain (all-purpose) flour	*4 tbsp*	*4 tbsp*	*4 tbsp*
plus			
ground ginger	*1–2 tsp*	*1–2 tsp*	*1–2 tsp*
or dried fruit	*1 tbsp*	*1 tbsp*	*1 tbsp*
or desiccated (shredded) coconut	*1 tbsp*	*1 tbsp*	*1 tbsp*

Equipment
Mixing bowl, rolling pin or milk bottle, baking tray

Cooking method
Top of stove, then oven

1 Turn on the oven, set at 375°F/190°C Gas Mark 5.
2 Smear some margarine over the base of a baking tray.
3 Put the sugar and margarine into a mixing bowl and beat them well together.
4 Beat in the egg
5 Mix in the flour, and any additional ingredients, to make a soft dough.
6 Sprinkle flour onto a work surface and roll out the dough to a thickness of 5mm/¹/₄in.
7 Cut into shapes, and lay these on the greased baking tray.

8 Brush the tops with milk and sprinkle on the topping.
9 Bake for 10–15 minutes.

temperature

If you are using an electric cooker, the temperature of the oven will be measured in degrees fahrenheit or celsius. Gas cookers have regulo marks ranging from $1/4$ to 9. An oven should be preheated to the right temperature before putting the food in. This will take 10–15 minutes, depending on the temperature setting.

	°Fahrenheit	°Celsius	Gas
Very low	225	110	$1/4$
	250	120	$1/2$
Low	275	140	1
	300	150	2
Moderate	325	160	3
	350	180	4
Moderately hot	375	190	5
	400	200	6
Hot	425	220	7
	450	230	8
Very hot	475	240	9

The controls that regulate the temperature of the rings on top of the stove are graded 1–5. If you are bringing something to the boil, you need to set the controls to 5. For simmering the heat needs to be as low as possible – 1 or even lower if your cooker has a $\frac{1}{2}$ grade. Stir-frying is done over a high heat at 5; frying 'over a medium/moderate heat' requires 2 or 3; for 'gentle' frying 1 would be sufficient.

the V s

vegetables

Like fruit, fresh vegetables are a good source of minerals, vitamins and fibre. In order to retain as many valuable nutrients as possible, don't overcook them or use too much water. Many vegetables can be eaten raw.

Fresh vegetables, particularly greens, should be eaten as soon as possible after buying them. Salad vegetables can be stored loosely wrapped in plastic bags in the salad drawer at the bottom of the refrigerator. Root vegetables will keep in a cool dark place for about a week. These should not be left in plastic bags because they will sweat and start to ferment.

Supermarkets now offer a selection of exotic vegetables from all over the world alongside the more familiar ones, so there is no reason why vegetables should be though of as 'boring'.

courgette bake

Servings: 1
Time to prepare: 1 hour

Ingredients	Metric	Imperial	American
courgettes (zucchini), cut into 1¹/₂in slices	2	2	2
oil	1 tbsp	1 tbsp	1 tbsp
spring onion (scallion), finely chopped	1	1	1
clove of garlic, peeled and crushed	1	1	1
tomatoes, sliced	2–3	2–3	2–3
grated Cheddar cheese	4 tbsp	4 tbsp	4 tbsp
salt and pepper			

Equipment
Frying pan (skillet), ovenproof dish, chopping board, sharp knife

Cooking method
Top of stove, then oven

1 Turn the oven on, set at 350°F/180°C Gas Mark 4.
2 Heat the oil in a frying pan (skillet) and gently fry the sliced courgettes (zucchini), onion and garlic for 10 minutes.
3 Add the tomatoes and cook for a further 5 minutes.
4 Season the mixture with salt and pepper.
5 Smear an ovenproof dish with a little butter and spoon half the courgette mixture into it.
6 Sprinkle with half the cheese.
7 Add the remaining courgettes and top with cheese.
8 Bake in the oven for 45 minutes.

stuffed peppers

Servings: 1
Time to prepare: 45 minutes

Ingredients

	Metric	Imperial	American
small (bell) pepper	2	2	2
oil	1 tbsp	1 tbsp	1 tbsp
small onion, peeled and sliced	1	1	1
minced (ground) beef	100g	4oz	1/2 cup
tomato purée (paste)	1 tbsp	1 tbsp	1 tbsp
cooked rice or breadcrumbs	2 tbsp	2 tbsp	2 tbsp
mixed dried herbs	1/2 tsp	1/2 tsp	1/2 tsp
salt and pepper			
grated Cheddar cheese	1 tbsp	1 tbsp	1 tbsp

Equipment
Saucepan, ovenproof dish, frying pan (skillet)

1 Turn on the oven, set at 350°F/180°C Gas Mark 4.
2 Put the pepper(s) into a saucepan, cover with boiling water and simmer for 1 minute.
3 Allow to cook, then slice off the top and remove the core and seeds.
4 Heat the oil and gently fry the onion and beef until the meat is brown.
5 Add the other ingredients and mix well.
6 Spoon the mixture into the peppers and stand them in an ovenproof dish.
7 Sprinkle grated cheese on top.
8 Cook for 35 minutes, until the cheese is brown and bubbly.

ratatouille

Servings: 2
Time to prepare: 1 hour

Served with brown rice or crusty wholemeal bread and cheese, this makes an excellent vegetarian meal. These ingredients will make enough for two servings – the second portion can be reheated for another meal. The aubergine (eggplant) is sprinkled with salt before cooking to remove excess moisture and any bitter taste. It is not absolutely essential, but does make the ratatouille taste better.

Ingredients	Metric	Imperial	American
small aubergine (eggplant), cut into 1cm/¹/₂in slices	*1*	*1*	*1*
oil	*1 tbsp*	*1 tbsp*	*1 tbsp*
onion, peeled and sliced	*1*	*1*	*1*
cloves of garlic, peeled and crushed	*2*	*2*	*2*
large courgette (zucchini), washed and cut into 1cm/¹/₂in slices	*1*	*1*	*1*
green (bell) pepper, sliced	*¹/₂*	*¹/₂*	*¹/₂*
tomatoes, chopped	*2*	*2*	*2*
mixed dried herbs	*¹/₂ tsp*	*¹/₂ tsp*	*¹/₂ tsp*
salt and pepper			

Equipment
Frying pan (skillet) or large saucepan with lid, chopping board, sharp knife, sieve

Cooking method
Top of stove

1 Put the sliced aubergine (eggplant) into a sieve and sprinkle with salt.
2 Leave to drain for 10–15 minutes, then dry the slices by pressing them between two pieces of kitchen paper.
3 Heat the oil over a medium heat and gently fry the aubergine (eggplant), onion, garlic, green pepper and courgettes (zucchini) for 5 minutes.
4 Add the tomatoes and dried herbs, and season with salt and pepper.
5 Cover with a lid and cook gently for about 45 minutes, until all the vegetables are broken down and soft.

• Stir-frying is a good way of cooking green vegetables, such as cabbage and chinese leaves. Shred the leaves finely and cook quickly in very hot oil. Sprinkle with soya sauce before serving.
• Cauliflour and leeks taste good in cheese sauce (see page 50)

vitamins

It should not be necessary to supplement your diet with vitamin pills. Provided you vary your diet and don't overcook your food so that vitamins are destroyed, you should be getting enough. Vitamins B and C cannot be stored in the body, so you need to eat foods that contain them every day. These are the main vitamins that we need, and the foods they are found in.

Vitamin	Necessary for	Found in
A	*Healthy eyes and skin*	*Meat, liver, kidney, oily fish, dairy products, carrots, tomatoes, green vegetables, oranges*
B	*Nervous system – deficiency causes depression and fatigue*	*Whole grain cereals, yeast, vegetable extract (eg Marmite) liver, lean meat, bacon, pulses, eggs, fish, milk, cheese*
C	*General health – deficiency causes depression and fatigue; unhealthy skin*	*Citrus fruits, blackcurrants, tomatoes, fresh green vegetables*
D	*Bones and teeth – it helps the absorption of calcium and phosphorus*	*Meat, liver, kidney, oily fish, dairy products, eggs*

the Y s

yoghurt

Yoghurt is an ideal dessert, quick snack or breakfast. There are all kinds of fancy yoghurts and yoghurt-based products available now – from very low-fat to the rich and creamy or custardy types. Natural plain yoghurt is simply milk to which 'yoghurt' cultures have been added. It is a useful ingredient for salads, and a healthy substitute for cream in many hot and cold dishes. If you eat a lot of yoghurt, it is worth making your own. All you need is a wide-mouthed vacuum flask. The ½ltr/1pt size is the most suitable.

making yoghurt

Milk must be sterilized for making yoghurt, so it is easier to use long-life, which has already been sterilized. (Fresh milk has to be brought to boiling point and then allowed to cool, all of which takes more time.) You can use full-cream, semi-skimmed or skimmed milk – the richer the milk, the thicker the yoghurt. You can also make a thicker yoghurt by adding 1–2 tablespoons of skimmed milk powder.

You need	Metric	Imperial	American
long-life milk	*¹/₂ltr*	*1pt*	*2¹/₂ cups*
plain yoghurt (not pasturised)	*1 tbsp*	*1 tbsp*	*1 tbsp*
skimmed milk powder	*2 tbsp*	*2 tbsp*	*2 tbsp*

1 Put the yoghurt and skimmed milk powder into a bowl and mix thoroughly together to make a smooth paste.
2 Heat the milk in a saucepan until it is lukewarm. (Dip your finger in to test – it should feel comfortable enough for you to leave your finger there.)
3 Stir the warm milk gradually into the yoghurt paste.
4 Pour into a clean flask and leave for about 6 hours, until the yoghurt has set.
5 Empty the yoghurt out into a container with a lid and store it in the refrigerator. It should stay fresh for 4–5 days.
6 Use a spoonful of the yoghurt to make the next batch.

things to add to yoghurt

Muesli and chopped banana: Makes a quick healthy breakfast.
Fresh fruit: Plain yoghurt is the ideal topping for strawberries, raspberries, or a mixture of chopped fresh fruit.
Fruit preserves: These contain more fruit and less sugar than traditional jam. Stir a spoonful into your home-made yoghurt.
Honey and toasted flaked almonds: Dribble the honey on top, then sprinkle with almonds. Particularly delicious with Greek yoghurt.

INDEX